Quotes and Testi

CW00351674

"This book bristles with energy, ideas and ~~_____ _____ __ _____~~ sense. The simple messages of taking control and making it happen – with practical steps to help get there – make this a must-read book. Overall Steve Connell outlines a clear and sensible framework, written in a down to earth and honest style, which shows how anyone can squeeze more out of life and work."

Fred Ford, Divisional Director, Chelsea Building Society

"This book takes you step by step through Steve's unique and thought provoking approach to maximising your potential, and what's more it is a thoroughly entertaining read. Whether you think you already have a very strong Personal Brand Essence or this is an entirely new concept to you – this guide is a must."

Fraser Longden, Group Head of Talent and Engagement, Kingfisher

"I have been fortunate to have had Steve as both a friend and a mentor for some years. This book captures perfectly both his easy style and challenging thinking that has helped me so much. It is both intentionally provocative and yet straight-forward to follow. Like Steve himself, it can be relied on to guide, to boost and to focus. It is indeed, inspirational."

Pete Westall, Retail Director, Mid Counties Co-Operative

"Here is a book that is highly relevant to all of us as we reach the various crossroads in life, whether it is leaving full time education, changing jobs or careers or charting a new path on retirement. Steve Connell takes us on a very personal and important journey in understanding how we can be better equipped to meet the challenges of the work place and life generally. Reading this book has the potential to both enhance and change your life."

John Dean, Chief Executive, British Shops and Stores Association

"I wish I'd read this when I was 18 and starting my career in retail. Over the years my personal brand essence has never really figured and therefore I have committed many of the failings Steve talks about in the book. I have read the book over a few long train journeys to work meetings and each time I've put it down I have a new spring in my step. A great book and an absolute must read for managers who want a successful career."

Kevin Breese, General Manager, Harvey Nichols

"Steve Connell is an inspiring force of nature. If you can't get to him in person, get his book."

Martin Butler, Retail Lecturer and Author

"Steve has a natural ability to connect to any individual at any level with a sense of urgency to match. I can recommend not only Steve but also his book. Better still combine the two!"

Peter Mallinson, Chief Executive, Multiyork

"A thoroughly enjoyable read. Steve introduces and expands upon ideas in a personable and intimate way without being intrusive."

Phil Ludgate, RBC Dexia

"Steve's strength is his own personal brand, his style and his passion. That's all very well when you're with him in person. It's a different challenge altogether when you've got to get this level of emotional engagement from a book. So, has he achieved it? I suggest strongly you read it...you won't be disappointed."

Jonathan Field, Managing Director, John Lewis Brent Cross

"It is rare that you find a book that is as fast paced and enjoyable as a holiday novel but yet has the potential to have a profound and positive impact on your life."

Steve Clarke, Global Head of Sales, BT Unilever

"This is a great read. Although I find it very difficult to come up with a single word that encompasses my "brand", I did find the book thought provoking (and believe me very few books manage to do that). What I particularly liked was the fact it wasn't all theory and fads. The fact that Steve's personal experiences permeate every chapter helps to make it a lot more real and will certainly engage the reader."

Dave Meckin, Managing Director, Insight Financial Consulting

PERSONAL BRAND ESSENCE

Steve Connell

2000

First published in 2009 by Management Books 2000 Ltd
Forge House, Limes Road
Kemble, Cirencester
Gloucestershire, GL7 6AD, UK
Tel: 0044 (0) 1285 771441
Fax: 0044 (0) 1285 771055
Email: info@mb2000.com
Web: www.mb2000.com

British Library Cataloguing in Publication Data is available

ISBN 9781852525828

For Claire.
My inspiration.

Contents

Summary

Imagine being able to define who you are, where you are going and how you will know when you have arrived.

That is the purpose of this book. To provoke you to think about who you are and what you stand for. To provoke you to think about how your behaviours create and reinforce perceptions in others. To provoke you to treat yourself as a brand in order to realise your own unique potential.

And why is this important? Because of what it enables you to do. It enables you to take control of your own destiny and provides you with a sense of purpose and direction. It enables you to stand out from the crowd and to differentiate your offer from that of others. It enables you to achieve the goals that you have set for yourself and to succeed both personally and professionally.

Preface

"If you don't know where you are going then any road will do."
From Alice's Adventures in Wonderland by Lewis Carroll

Think of a business, any company will do, it doesn't have to be a global conglomerate.

Now imagine for a moment how much money that business spends on developing its brand. On defining its niche in the market, its competitive points of differentiation. More or less than you earn?

Now, if time were money ask yourself this. How much do you spend on developing your brand? Defining your forte? Identifying your unique points of differentiation. Probably much less than you earn. Perhaps nothing at all.

The good news is that you are not alone. Hardly anybody does. After all, we're not too good at that 'navel gazing thing' anyway, or at coming up with what it is that we really excel at, let alone making a big noise about it.

But that's my point. No self-respecting business would go to market without defining its brand, what it stood for or why we should buy it – not if it wanted to stay in business anyway. So why should we? It's a competitive market place out there. We need to be very clear about who we are, what we want and what people can expect to get from us. We owe it to ourselves to do the best that we can for ourselves. To make a difference. To realise our full potential, both in our careers and our personal lives.

The aim of this book is to provoke you. To get you to think about the answers to these questions. To provide you with some structure, some kind of plan to help you realise your personal goals and business ambitions. You'll have a head start on the rest at the very least.

The problem with not having a plan is that you don't have any idea of where you are going, what you are trying to achieve or of knowing that you have arrived. The danger is that we go round and around on the merry-go-round, often enjoying the journey but ultimately ending up right back where we started. If we have a plan then at least we have a sense of purpose, a feeling as to the general direction in which we should be heading. This helps us to make good decisions and allows us to refine the plan to take account of changes in our circumstances.

For many years I didn't have a plan. I coasted through school, not being certain at all of what I wanted to ultimately achieve in life. I remember having some romantic notion of being a lawyer, stimulated primarily by the American TV series Petrocelli and by the prospect of the money that that sort of career would provide. I underachieved at school and consoled myself with the fact that with 3 million people unemployed in the early eighties having any sort of job was an achievement. After all, I wasn't that concerned about what I did as long as I had enough beer money and the flexibility to play rugby.

As a Gloucester boy, rugby was central to my existence and my raison d'être was rugby, beer and women, though not necessarily in that order – it did depend on which day of the week it was. I fell into a job with BT or British Telecommunications, as it was then called, and initially I was just delighted to have a job and to be earning an income. My career developed, after a fashion, and I moved steadily (that's business speak for slowly) up the corporate ladder one small rung at a time, usually through luck rather than judgement. With time the rate at which I moved through the rungs quickened as I began to form more of an idea about what I wanted to achieve. I became more self-aware and conscious of the weaknesses that I needed to address as well as the strengths that I needed to hone. I began to develop a network of confidants, mentors and sponsors. I began to form more of an opinion about how things should be done. Gradually, I started to feel that I was more in control of where I was going and what I wanted to achieve. With that control came confidence. Confidence in the validity of my ideas and conviction in the belief that I had in myself.

When I created *inspire* in 2004 I began to explore these notions in more detail. Many of the programmes that I offer through the company are predicated on the concept of greater self-awareness, self-belief and personal development. I provoke people to think about their attitude.

I looked around for inspiration myself. I looked for books which would help me to articulate what I meant to my audience and I soon realised that there was a paucity of information on the subject. What help and advice I could find was scattered through a handful of books and what they all seemed to lack, to me at least, was anything tangible that the reader could do to address the valid provocation that you need to know more about yourself in order to be in control of your ultimate destiny.

That is why I wrote this book. I wanted to provide people with a framework for developing their own plan. I wanted to provoke people to think about what they were trying to achieve and how they were going to set about doing it. I wanted to write the book that I was looking for. The book that I wish I had read when I was twenty-three, rather than wrote when I was forty-three.

Steve Connell
Puerto Pollensa

Foreword

By Stan Kaufman

Making the most of your life is something, I guess, we all want to do. Of course, this means different things to different people but starting with the answer and working backwards to see how you get there seems to me a pretty smart thing to do.

In his zany but highly witty series, *The Hitchhikers Guide to the Galaxy*, Douglas Adams tells us in the first of five books that the answer to the Great Question of Life, the Universe and Everything is … Forty-two!

However, other than telling us on Page 2 that inscribed on the cover of the Guide is the advice DON'T PANIC we never get a clear picture of how to move from the answer to the question … or vice versa.

In this respect this is where Steve's book is different. Not that Steve intends for us to be consumed with panic but rather he plots a very carefully considered path that leads to our chosen destination. Human beings aren't like machines; we don't come with an Operating Manual. Yet, in a way, this is exactly what Steve helps us to create. Our very own customised, tailor made Operating Manual.

When reviewing a book, Dorothy Parker once famously said, "This is not a book that should be cast lightly aside, it should be hurled with great force!"

Well I think the first part of Dottie P's observations apply equally to Steve's work … it certainly shouldn't be cast lightly aside. However, in this case, the great force exerted should be channelled in putting into practice the various elements of Steve's master plan.

I have known Steve Connell for over 15 years. I have seen him develop into a truly outstanding person both in his professional and in his private life. He has always been a great force of nature…an energetic, dynamic, larger than life character. With Steve you never have been in any doubt that the glass is half full rather than half empty.

Steve has a great generosity of spirit and it's that very generosity that made him a truly outstanding manager and makes him such an inspirational coach. Steve generously and courageously shares his journey with us so that we can understand ourselves better and recognise what's really important to us – thus helping us to achieve a more fulfilling life.

About the author

Steve Connell was born on 30th November 1964. The eldest of five children, he grew up in Gloucester studying at the Crypt Grammar School. To be fair, 'studying' is too theatrical a word. Steve's headmaster, Michael Holmes, noted in one of his earlier school reports that "Connell's potential is being hampered somewhat by his frequent bouts of freewheeling". This is perhaps a fairer description of young Mr. Connell's attitude and, whilst he managed to secure himself a position at BT, his oft-stated lofty ambitions were not sufficiently backed up with much in the way of application.

Having spent ten years or so in various administrative roles within BT, his career took a more dynamic turn when injury brought to an end any preposterous thoughts he had of an England rugby career.

Steve became the Store Manager at BT's 'Phone Shop' in Bristol and within a year he was the General Store Manager of the new flagship store that opened on Oxford Street in the early nineties. During this time Steve became involved with the British Shops and Stores Association (bssa) annual Summer School at Keble College in Oxford, attending as a delegate in 1992 and subsequently as a Group Director for the first time in 1994. His involvement with the retail sector continued as he project managed the joint venture between Dixons Stores Group (DSGi) and BT which became known as The Link, DSGi's fourth high street retail chain.

Following stints in Account Management and the marketing department, Steve ultimately became a sales sector General Manager with BT and, at around the same time, Chairman of the bssa Summer School having served as a Group Director for eight years and as Vice Chairman for two.

Steve created *inspire*, a management development consultancy in 2004. The consultancy focuses on the delivery of development programmes to talent pools identified by clients, one to one coaching and conference speaking. Steve specialises in the subjects of Personal Brand Essence and Business to Business account management.

Introduction

"Life is like a wild Tiger. You can either lie down and let it lay its paw on your head – or sit on its back and ride it."
Indian proverb

Who is this book for?

It would be trite of me to say that this book is for everyone. There are numerous people for whom the provocations contained herein are not relevant. Equally though, there are many people whom I believe would benefit immensely from considering what their brand says about themselves and how they are perceived by others.

I have found that teenagers and students are less moved to take action as a result of hearing the provocations that I will expand upon in this book. They are still young and, as a rule, have not yet experienced a great deal in their brief lives. They therefore have little context with which to compare and contrast and have still to make up their mind and form opinions on many things. Good luck to them I say. They have to find their own way and learn from their own mistakes as their journey unfolds. But have a plan, some idea of where you are going, so that you do not waste any precious time. Oh to be young again, but with the spectacular advantage of being that age along with the battle scars that those of us who are twice their age now sport.

There comes a time in everyone's life, I think when we become twenty-something, when we begin to get some context and perspective. We have already tried and failed or tried and succeeded, perhaps in our attempts to get into university, in a personal relationship or in gaining promotion at work. We know what is important to us and we have a much better idea of what we want to achieve with our lives. We are ready to define our plan.

As we enter our thirties the die is often cast. We are probably in a relationship and we have, if not a career, then a job at the very least. We know who we are, although we may find it difficult to articulate that clearly, and we know what we like. We have a circle of family and friends, we have a business network and we have probably decided on the general tenor and direction of our lives. We have an opportunity to refine our plan.

By the time we are forty our job has become our career and our children have become our legacy. We are over half way through the adventure and have already ticked off many things that we wanted to do. But we are growing more conscious of the clock ticking, the hourglass being fuller at the bottom than at the top. We notice when the clock strikes midnight and count the chimes because we know that another day has gone and that time is running out. We can see the horizon of retirement more clearly now and we have a good idea of how that will look and feel. But we still have time. Time to achieve those things that are still on the list and to ensure that we do indeed get everything that we wanted from life. Time to exceed our aspirations and ultimately realise our full potential. We have an opportunity to distil the plan one final time.

So, this book is for anyone who wants to understand and improve themselves. For anyone who is remotely interested in what other people think of them. For anyone who believes that they can achieve more in life.

Why you should read this book?

This book is designed to provoke you to take action and to furnish you with a framework with which to implement that action plan. I aim to provide you with some ideas that will help you to define who you are, identify what is important to you and what motivates you as well as what you need to do in order to achieve both your personal and professional ambitions. It is my hope that you will pause and reflect as you read the book. Keep a notebook and pencil handy and record your answers to any of the provocations that resonate with you. Ultimately the book will enable you to identify your Personal Brand Essence and the behaviours that need to be associated with it. However, we need to do the groundwork first and fashion a plan and a promise to ourselves before we can create the performance.

How the book is laid out

This book is laid out in three sections. The beginning looks at 'The Plan' and asks you why you need to do anything in the first place. It explains what I mean by Personal Brand Essence. It asks you to do some self-analysis and find out what people think of you. It offers some tips on successful personal development and provokes you to identify your goals in life and create a development plan that enables you to achieve those goals.

The middle of the book focuses on 'The Promise'. This is the promise of action that you will take as a result of understanding yourself and your aims in life more fully. The 'So What?' test. It asks you some questions about how you are shaping your career and what you are renowned for. It stimulates you to define your Personal Brand Essence, become more self-aware and understand how your behaviours and actions are perceived by others.

The end of the book concentrates on 'The Performance', how you go about implementing your plan. It looks at how you project your brand to your different audiences. It helps you to identify the behaviours that you need to modify and develop in order to reinforce the brand that you have defined. It prompts you to think about your style, your attitude and your appearance, all of which have a huge influence on how you are perceived by others. It helps you to build your personal network and to create personal impact.

Section 1
The Plan

So what do you need to do?

This section of the book explores brand and explains what I mean by Personal Brand Essence. It asks you to do some self-analysis and find out what people think of you. It offers some tips on successful personal development and provokes you to identify your goals in life and create a development plan that enables you to achieve those goals.

1

What is brand?

"A brand for a company is like a brand for a person.
You earn reputation by trying to do hard things well."
Jeff Bezos

The Oxford English Dictionary defines the word brand as a particular make of goods, an identifying trade mark or label. A special characteristic that impresses unforgettably on one's mind. It also makes reference to branding irons and the branding of livestock. It intrigues me as to what came first, the use of the word 'brand' in the business context or the use of the word in the more agricultural sense of marking one's possessions indelibly with the owner's mark. My guess is the latter, given that the use of the word dates back to the times of slavery. No coincidence then, that the word has become so intrinsically linked with how it is used in business. A brand is a mark, etched upon the product produced by the company. Yes, a logo, but it says so much more than the product or the logo does.

It signifies pride. Pride in the mark that you put on your produce. It tells the prospective buyer that when they buy the product that they are buying more than the item itself. Martin Butler, former chief at the advertising agency RPM3 and now an author and lecturer, summarised this brilliantly in the title of his first book, *People Don't Buy What You Sell, They Buy What You Stand For.*

Brand is the cornerstone of any business. It defines the company and provides clarity and a sense of purpose for its employees. It is the guiding principle that enables the business to steer its course. The brand of a business tells its people and its customers what the company stands for.

Branding is central to the concept of marketing. Philip Kotler, regarded by many as the Godfather of Marketing, contends that; "The art of marketing is largely the art of brand building. When something is not a brand it will probably be viewed as a commodity." This is because it has no context. It does not pick up the story from where the last product left off.

Everything that a company produces and delivers into the market place reinforces the perceptions that we have of that company. Its brand. What it represents.

Kotler goes further in helping us to understand brand and how it is created. I'm a great believer in keeping things simple. If someone has developed a model or a concept or a theory that works then why change it or attempt to add to it? The result is often over complexity that leads to confusion. As you will see in Chapter 3, I have shamelessly used Kotler's framework as the basis for how one defines Personal Brand Essence.

Kotler contends that a brand can convey up to six levels of meaning.

Attributes

Brands bring to mind certain attributes. They are often the tangible elements of a brand. They manifest themselves through the people, the products and the look and feel of its points of interaction with its customers.

Benefits

A brand is more than just a set of attributes. Customers are not buying the attributes, they are buying the personal benefits that the product provides for them at an emotional level.

Values

The brand tells us what the business stands for. What its values are. These values are projected in order to attract people who aspire to or share those values.

Culture

The brand may also represent a certain cultural heritage associated with the business. The history, tradition and prestige that this culture represents also acts as an attraction.

Personality

The brand can project a certain kind of personality. This may be a person who is associated with the company or the sort of people who work for it, buy from it or are used to advertise and promote it.

User

The brand suggests the kind of consumer who buys or uses the product. The users will be those who respect the values, culture and personality of the product.

Over the years I have worked with many people on the development of their Personal Brand Essence. I always start with the same question – What is brand?

For me this is part of the beauty of brands. It is such a subjective topic that everyone has a differing view and opinion. Having said that, I have found that the same words are consistently used to describe how people define brand.

- *Integrity* – Does the brand do what it says it will do?
- *Quality* – Is the brand worth the money?
- *Image* – What does the brand say about me if I use it?
- *Status* – Will the brand help me to be seen in a better light by others?
- *Reputation* – Is the brand consistent with how I want to be seen?
- *Promise* – What is it that the brand is offering me?

- *Behaviour* – Does the brand behave consistently?
- *Symbolism* – Does the brand look good and make me look good as a result?
- *Aspiration* – How does the brand show that I am achieving and succeeding?
- *Values* – Do I like what the brand stands for?
- *Personality* – Am I happy being associated with other people with whom the brand is associated?
- *Differentiate* – Does the brand allow me to distinguish myself from others?
- *Identity* – Does the brand support my individuality?
- *Beliefs* – Do my beliefs match those that I perceive of the brand?
- *Perception* – Will others see me as I want to be seen by using the brand?
- *Emotion* – How will I feel by using the brand?

The next question I ask of people is to identify a business brand that they feel is most closely representative of them.

Why don't you try this now? Take a moment to think of the brand that you feel is most synonymous with you. Not necessarily the brand that you 'like' the most but the brand that you would say you have most in common with. Test out your thoughts on a friend of colleague.

Many people find identifying a single business brand a difficult to do. After all, it is a highly subjective topic. Some people love certain brands and are very happy to associate themselves with them whilst others see the same brands as an anathema and would be horrified at the thought of being connected with them. Most of us see great positives in some brands but are also aware of some of the negatives associated with that brand and would not want those negatives to be linked with us.

Some people wrestle with the dilemma of choosing a brand that is currently representative of themselves with selecting one that it more reflective of how they would like to be seen now and in the future. This is actually quite useful because if we can distinguish what the differences between the perceptions of the two brands are, we have a starting point for some of the work that we need to do to close the gap.

The truth is, of course, that we are not a single business brand, nor indeed a combination of several brands. We are 'Me Plc', our own brand.

I believe that brand is all about emotion. It is emotion based upon how we feel about the brand. The perception that we have formed of the brand has to be constantly reinforced through the behaviour of the brand. Every interaction has to be consistent with that emotion or our perception of the brand will begin to change.

We all recognise the critical importance and value of branding to all organisations. My provocation is this. If you were to re-read this chapter and replace the words 'company', 'business' or 'organisation' with the word 'you' would it read any differently? Would any of the content be less relevant to you as an individual?

What is your promise? What is the emotion that you are trying to create in others? How do you want to be perceived by others? We all have a personal brand that creates emotion in others. It forges their perceptions of us and how we behave either reinforces or changes those perceptions.

Brand is emotion.
It is created by attitudes, perceptions and beliefs.
It manifests itself in consistent behaviours which reinforce
that emotion.

Brand can convey up to six levels of meaning:

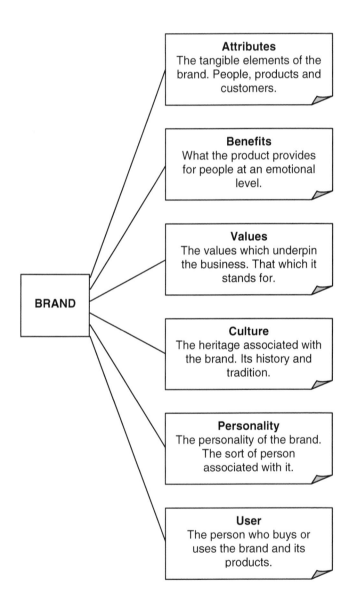

Attributes
The tangible elements of the brand. People, products and customers.

Benefits
What the product provides for people at an emotional level.

Values
The values which underpin the business. That which it stands for.

BRAND

Culture
The heritage associated with the brand. Its history and tradition.

Personality
The personality of the brand. The sort of person associated with it.

User
The person who buys or uses the brand and its products.

So What?

- Brand is emotion. It is emotion based upon how we feel about the brand. The perception that we have formed of the brand has to be constantly reinforced through the behaviour of the brand. Every interaction has to be consistent with that emotion or our perception of the brand will begin to change.

- That being the case then it makes sense to ask some searching questions of ourselves:
    - What is our personal promise?
    - How do we want to be perceived by others?
    - What emotions do we want to create in others?
    - How consistent are our behaviours with the perceptions that we are trying to create?

2

Why do people buy brands?

"One's philosophy is not best expressed in words; it's expressed in the choices that we make. In the long run, we shape our lives and we shape ourselves. The process never ends until we die. And the choices that we make are ultimately our responsibility."
Eleanor Roosevelt

We can all reel off the names of the powerhouse brands, those that are globally recognised, the likes of Coca Cola and Microsoft, IBM and General Electric, Intel and Nokia but have you ever stopped to think more deeply about these brands, what the names actually mean to you?

What do they say to you? Who and what do you associate them with? How do they make you feel?

It's difficult, isn't it? It's highly subjective and based almost entirely upon our own values, perceptions and experiences. It's intangible and that is why it is so hard to value a brand. How do you put a value on the way that you feel about something?

The same applies, of course, to the other brands that we choose to use. We choose them because they also say something about us. They are representative of us because other people see us using them and form an opinion of us as a result.

Admittedly, this is often at a sub-conscious level perhaps driven by convenience and accessibility but nevertheless we will make many proactive decisions when it comes to choosing a brand. Whether it be a dishwasher or a car, a suit or a sofa, a handbag or a set of golf clubs, our choices are formed based upon our perceptions of the brand. We will take into account reliability, quality and price, but we are also egocentrically aware of image, status and appearance.

In fact, price is a misnomer. Price has very little to do with our brand purchasing decisions. There are occasions when, admittedly, price can sometimes be the overriding factor. Take insurance or petrol, for instance. We tend to buy on price because the purchase is commodity based and brand has little or nothing to do with the purchase. But where perception is involved, ours or others, then brand does play a part.

Affordability is, of course, an issue but the main decision making criterion is based around value and not price. What will we get for our money? Think about the house or apartment in which you live. You could have got one for less money but you chose to buy or rent the one that you have for a number of reasons. Location, space, aspect and reputation of the neighbourhood.

Ask yourself about the last car that you bought. Did you spend more than £5000 on it? Why, when you could have bought one for £500? Because it gave you more of what you wanted, in terms of reliability, safety and looks. It said something about you and the brand of car that you chose said even more.

This brand perception factor doesn't just apply on large purchases either. Where do you buy your clothes? Which supermarket gets your custom? Where do you sun yourself each year? Your answers to all of these provocations say something about you. About how you see yourself and how you would like others to see you.

Many people say that they buy things because they need them. I take issue with this on the whole. After all, if you needed a pair of shoes you could make them using some discarded carpet remnants and a length of string, rather than buying a pair of Jimmy Choo's.

If you needed to eat you could grow your own vegetables and sift through the bargain bins rather than cram your shopping trolley at your favourite supermarket with luxuries and treats and then throw one third of it away at the end of the week.

If you needed a holiday you could pack your rucksack, strap on your tent and set off for the beautiful English countryside rather than head for the beaches and the bars of the Costa's.

If you needed to get from A to B you might invest in a bus pass or a bicycle rather than a car. Even if you did buy a car you could get one for fifty quid if you really looked around. Granted, it may not look great or be the most reliable of runners but it would get you from A to B just as well as the latest production line model.

As a rule people do not buy things because they need them. They buy things because they want them. People tend to buy things for emotional reasons. These emotions tend to be driven by fear, profit or flattery.

People choose to buy insurance because they are afraid that something may go wrong. Insurance companies prey on this emotion of fear and create scenarios based upon what would you do if this happened or that happened. People choose to buy personal belongings that enable them to keep up with the Jones's because they are concerned about what other people may think of them if they are not part of the latest trend or craze.

People choose to buy stocks and shares and investment policies because they hope to make money on them in the long run. People choose to buy property, not just to live in, but to turn into positive equity and feather their nest for the future.

People choose to buy the latest fashions because it tells others that they have their finger on the pulse and can afford to look good. People choose to holiday in exotic, chic and exclusive locations because it says that they have worked hard and that they deserve to reward themselves.

None of this is wrong. Many of the examples I have laid out above are very relevant to the work I will ask you to do in Chapter 6 when we look at your Personal Life Plan and the personal goals that you have set for yourself. People, quite rightly, aspire to move onwards and upwards, to achieve greater things in life and to reward themselves and their loved ones for the hard yards they have put in.

What is important is that we understand how important brand is in creating perceptions. In the same way that you or I will have a perception, a feeling, an opinion about a product or a company, so the same applies to people.

There is an old saying that you can't choose your family, but that you can choose your friends. The question has to be, why do we choose the people that we do to be our friends? Why do they choose us?

Because we like them, yes, but let's get deeper than that. Why do we like them? Because their characteristics and behaviours attract us, we enjoy their company, they make us laugh, they understand how we think. They appeal to what motivates us and the same must apply for them to like us.

In a business context the evaluation criterion is similar. You will almost certainly work for the company that you do because you feel an association with that company. You like what they stand for and the opportunities that they present to you. You enjoy the work and the people with whom you work.

The feeling is mutual. They employed you because they liked you and they felt that you would be a good fit for their culture. You had the right skills and aptitude for the job but it was your attitudinal traits that appealed to them most. You would make a difference to their performance and add something to the organisation.

It is that 'something' that I would like to help you to try and define.

Have you achieved everything that you could have done? Have you pushed your way up the corporate ladder? Have your ambitions been fully met? Or, are others moving past you? Are you being overlooked? Are your capabilities not being recognised?

That 'something' is your brand. In the same way that we choose brands so do people choose us, whether that be personally or professionally. Our challenge is to understand for ourselves what that brand is and then live it, consciously and proactively.

So What?

- People do not buy things because they need them. Nor are they overly concerned with the price of things.

- People buy brands for one of three emotional reasons. They want to make a profit, overcome a fear or flatter themselves.

- Employers buy into people not just because they have the right skills and aptitude for the job, but also because they demonstrate the right attitude. They buy into them because they think that they will make a difference to their organisation.

3

What is Personal Brand Essence?

*"The greatest human freedom is the freedom to choose
one's attitude."*
Viktor Frankel

I have great news for you. You are being sent on a six month sabbatical. You are being offered the chance to go on a round the world trip to recharge your batteries and add to your life experiences at the same time. You can go alone or take anyone you would like to with you. All of your expenses are covered and you have the full blessing of your company. In fact it was their idea in the first place as they know that you will come back refreshed, invigorated and wiser as a result.

There is only one condition. You must recruit someone to do your job, to the standards that you currently attain, while you are away. You have to write a job advert for your current position and describe the attributes that the individual that you employ will need to have.

You are guaranteed to get your job back on your return, but if the person with whom you have temporarily replaced yourself does not live up to your employer's expectations then you will have to repay all of the costs of your trip.

Now, I know this sort of opportunity comes up all of the time, but bear with me. I need to try and make a point.

Go on. Write down all of the attributes that you think this individual will need to have in order to do your job as well as you do.

Let's compare lists. I would guess that yours will contain many, if not all of the following:

- Highly motivated
- Hits the floor running
- Honest
- Loyal
- Technically proficient
- Ambitious
- People person
- Network of contacts
- Reliable
- Conscientious
- Communicator
- Industry knowledge
- Flexibility

- Demonstrates leadership
- Quick learner
- Delegates effectively
- High energy
- Sound commercial awareness
- Discreet
- Professional

Now I would like you to decide whether the attributes that you have listed are skill based or attitudinal. In other words, if the attribute can be taught and learnt it is a skill, if it is inherently part of the individuals make up then it is attitudinal.

Let's look at my list and add an 'A' for an attitudinal attribute and an 'S' for a skills based attribute.

•	Highly motivated	**A**
•	Hits the floor running	**A/S**
•	Honest	**A**
•	Loyal	**A**
•	Technically proficient	**S**
•	Ambitious	**A**
•	People person	**A/S**
•	Network of contacts	**S**
•	Reliable	**A**
•	Conscientious	**A**
•	Communicator	**A/S**
•	Industry knowledge	**S**
•	Flexibility	**A**
•	Demonstrates leadership	**A/S**
•	Quick learner	**A/S**
•	Delegates effectively	**A/S**
•	High energy	**A**
•	Sound commercial awareness	**S**
•	Discreet	**A**
•	Professional	**A**

Notice anything? About eighty percent of the attributes listed are attitudinal. This doesn't mean that the skills attributes are any less important. They are fundamental. After all, motivated idiots are dangerous people to have around the place! What it does tell us is that eighty percent of what really counts is one's attitude. It has to be the starting point. Get the mind right and the rest will follow.

I have always contended, when recruiting people to join my teams, that if you give me someone with the right attitude we can teach them the skills they need to do the job well. And let us not underestimate the importance of skills. They are a critical ingredient in creating the ultimate performance that we will examine in more detail in the final chapters of this book.

As we know from Chapter 1, *The Oxford English Dictionary* defines brand as; 'a special characteristic that impresses unforgettably on one's mind'.

It also gives us a great insight to the meanings of words 'personal' and 'essence'.

Personal is defined as 'one's own, individual and private'.

Essence is defined as 'the indispensable quality or element identifying a thing or determining its character, fundamental, vital'. It comes from the Latin verb esse 'to be'.

By taking all three definitions we could define Personal Brand Essence, literally as; 'one's own individual, indispensable, identifying quality that impresses unforgettably on one's mind'.

Personal Brand Essence is the thing that defines you. It is your personal promise. It is the single thing that sets you apart from others. It is the essence, the last distilled drop that would remain if you boiled yourself down to the one single constituent that makes you, you.

It is your attitude. Your state of mind. It's fundamentally about choice. How you choose to be.

"Whether you think you can or whether you think you can't, then you are probably right," said Henry Ford.

By definition this means that your brand is the same whether you are at work, at home or out on the town with your friends. It just manifests itself in a slightly different way, through the way you choose to behave.

Now there is a sweeping statement! Many of the people that I work with take issue with this point of view. They believe that they are distinctly different people at home than they are at work. They contend that they, on occasion, behave in markedly different ways when at work than when they are socialising publicly or in the comfort of their own home.

I would agree that some of the behaviours might be slightly different but surely, fundamentally, you are the same person. You still have the same values and beliefs, the same principles and opinions, the same characteristics and personality. If not you would truly be schizophrenic and the question of who the real you is would be constantly raging in your mind.

A business would never go to market with a confused brand message, trying to say one thing to one audience and something else to another. Neither should we. Our brand is our brand whether we are at work, home or play and this is a very important part of understanding the importance of our Personal Brand Essence. If we miss this point and behave in ways that are entirely at odds with the brand perceptions that we are trying to create then our message becomes blurred and confusing and our brand starts to become tainted and damaged.

So what are the constituent parts of one's Personal Brand Essence? What are the building blocks? You will recall my own definition of brand from Chapter 1. That brand is an emotion. It is an emotion created by a perception that is formed, driven and reinforced through behaviours.

With due deference to Philip Kotler, I suggest that your Personal Brand Essence is made up of many of the same components that go into creating a business brand, but then personalised to provide relevant context.

As with Kotler's brand analysis, there are six component parts. They are attributes, benefits, values, experience, behaviours and personality. Let's take them one by one.

Attributes

Describe your physical characteristics, how you see yourself and how others see you. Large or small, tall or short, blonde or dark. Recall how others describe you. What words do they use? Beautiful, handsome, pretty or rugged. Elegant or informal. Imposing or inconspicuous. What is physically distinctive about you, that sets you apart from most others? What things would you like to change about your physical appearance? Don't be tempted to use words like 'plain' or 'average'. Get creative. Be expressive.

Benefits

Describe how people feel as a result of experiencing you as a person. Do they feel motivated, enthused and inspired? Do they feel warm and safe? Are they moved to take action by you? Are you a good confidant, helping them with their problems and to grow in confidence? What do people get from you? It is important that you don't just limit yourself to things that you know to be true, but also include some aspirational things in your list too. How would you like people to feel as a result of interacting with you?

Values

Which values are most important to you? Values such as integrity, honesty and fairness. These are often formed by your upbringing and your life experiences. We become more aware through these experiences of what we see as the rights and wrongs of the world. Try to list your values in order, making yourself prioritise them as you go otherwise you may end up with a long list of good words but be unable to articulate which ones are most important to you.

Experience

What do you know? What are you good at? What have you already done in your personal life and in your business career that you can evidence? This component is made up of your proven track record and the credibility that comes with it. Check your CV if you need a little inspiration. It will remind you of the jobs that you have done in the past and the capabilities that you needed to develop in order to do those jobs well.

Behaviours

What are the things that you say and do? Are your behaviours consistent? Think about how you behave when you are under pressure as well as when things are going well. Do you ever do or say things that, with the benefit of hindsight, you would not have said or done? Do you behave differently at home than at work? Do you behave differently when you are out on your own or with close friends than you do at home? If so, why?

Personality

What is it that makes you, you? What are your personality characteristics, traits and foibles? What are the words that you would use to describe your personality? How do those that know you describe your personality? Let me suggest a few words to get you going, but don't limit yourself to choosing from just these. Confident, caring, gregarious, cheerful, optimistic, fun, pugnacious, positive, adventurous, calm, quiet, serious, thoughtful, reflective, considerate, infectious, exciting, intoxicating, reserved. Again, don't create a great long list, try to distil it down to three or four that are most representative of you.

It will really help you to spend some time now working on these building blocks from a personal perspective. How would you describe your own attributes, benefits, values, experiences, behaviours and personality? When we come to defining your Personal Brand Essence in Chapter 10, the words that you have recorded here will be of great use and will give you a flying start.

Personal Brand Essence
'One's own individual, indispensable, identifying quality that impresses unforgettably on one's mind.'

One's Personal Brand consists of six components. These components are the foundations upon which our own Personal Brand Essence is constructed. They highlight our points of differentiation and ensure authenticity when we set about defining our Personal Brand Essence.

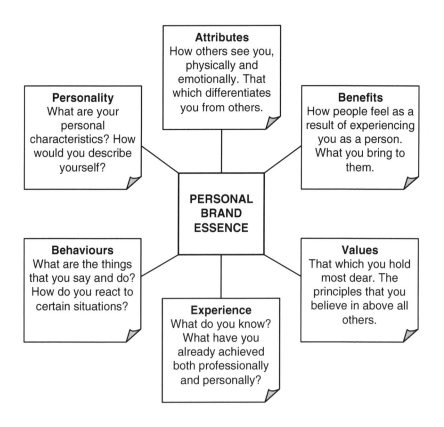

Attributes
How others see you, physically and emotionally. That which differentiates you from others.

Personality
What are your personal characteristics? How would you describe yourself?

Benefits
How people feel as a result of experiencing you as a person. What you bring to them.

PERSONAL BRAND ESSENCE

Behaviours
What are the things that you say and do? How do you react to certain situations?

Values
That which you hold most dear. The principles that you believe in above all others.

Experience
What do you know? What have you already achieved both professionally and personally?

So What?

- A business would never go to market with a confused brand message, trying to say one thing to one audience and something else to another. Neither should we. Our brand is our brand whether we are at work, home or play and this is a very important part of understanding the importance of our Personal Brand Essence. If we behave in ways that are at odds with the brand perceptions that we are trying to create then our message becomes confusing and our brand damaged.

- Personal Brand Essence is made up of six elements:
  1. Our personal attributes and characteristics
  2. The benefits that we bring to others
  3. Our values and beliefs
  4. The life experience we have gained
  5. The way that we choose to behave
  6. Our personality

4

Personal awareness analysis

"Because it is easier to say, 'I can't' than 'I can', or at least 'I can try' many people go through life unaware of untapped strength, even untapped ability. They haven't explored their own capabilities. They really don't know where their strength lies."
Eleanor Roosevelt

Be warned. We are not very good at this. After all, when was the last time that you sat down and undertook an extensive personal analysis on yourself? Never, is usually the answer. After all it's just not something that we do, not consciously or deliberately at least, but it is the essential starting point if we are to make a proactive and conscious attempt to improve ourselves.

Many people find it quite difficult to be totally honest with themselves. Some people are completely blind to their weaknesses and shortcomings and crash through life unaware or unconcerned about the implications of their actions. Others fool themselves into believing that they are better than they are, that they are already the finished article, that they have nothing more to learn. A few see little or no merit in themselves at all and as a result lack confidence, self-esteem and self-belief. The majority of people trust in their instinct and hope that fate will deal them a good hand. I contend that if we know what our strengths and weaknesses are we can be more in control of our own destiny. We can choose to take action.

One of Stephen Covey's *7 Habits of Highly Effective People* is to 'Begin with the end in mind'. When I was a child I used to be fascinated by the 'coffee break' pages in newspapers that my parents would pore over for hours. Cryptic crosswords with an alternative set of easy crosswords clues, where the answers were the same (a particular favourite of mine), number puzzles, spelling conundrums and mazes. Mazes fascinated me. I used to sit for what seemed like hours trying to work my way through the maze in my head or by tracing my finger along the lines before making a mark on the paper. It became a point of principle with me that once I had put pen to paper I had to get it right, just in case someone else happened to come across my work later in the day. Then it dawned on me. If I started from the centre of the maze there was only ever one way out and as long as I retraced my route whilst it was fresh in my mind, I could complete the task in seconds. I know it was a cheat but people were always very impressed with how quickly I could do it and that pleased me.

In the same way it is vital, when we are setting about improving ourselves and considering which turn to take next in our own maze that we have a pretty clear idea about where we ultimately want to end up. We need to be clear about the resources that we have at our disposal. We need to have a clear appreciation of what we are good at, what we can improve upon and what motivates us. We have to start with ourselves.

You may well be familiar with the acronym SWOT. It stands for Strengths, Weaknesses, Opportunities and Threats and is a frequently used tool in business. It is a commonly employed methodology, most often used to help identify what needs to happen next within an organisation. It is used to help formulate business strategy, gain competitive insight and plan tactical sales activity. It is a very effective tool for identifying the action that a business needs to take in order to take advantage of its competitive strengths and to address its weaknesses thereby maximising its opportunities and mitigating the threats that it faces.

It is also an exceptionally useful tool to apply to us as individuals.

Strengths and Weaknesses are internally focused. In other words, they apply to us. They set apart those things that we are good at and those that we are not so good at.

Opportunities and Threats are externally focused. In other words, they are the possible consequences of our strengths and weaknesses. They distinguish between the opportunities that may present themselves as a result of our strengths and the potential threats to us if we fail to address our weaknesses.

It is cause and effect. Because we are like this...the following could affect us.

List your strengths and prioritise the possible opportunities that could arise from them. List your weaknesses and prioritise the ensuing threats.

The following SWOT is an example to help guide you. The illustration lists a number of possible strengths and weaknesses that an individual may have. If those strengths listed were the case then, as an example, the corresponding role based opportunities may exist. If the weaknesses listed were evident then the potential threat to the ways other people perceive the individual may be relevant.

Once you have completed your own SWOT seek the contribution of one or two trusted friends and confidants, who will be open and honest with you. Ask them what they feel your strengths and weaknesses are and how your current behaviours affect their and others perception of you. They will keep you honest and also help you to prioritise the action that you need to take.

Strengths

- People person
- Attention to detail
- Reliability
- Communication skills
- Motivational
- Empathetic
- Creative
- Planning and organisation

Opportunities

- A people management role
- A role where meeting deadlines is imperative
- A role where trust and integrity are paramount
- A role that requires the creation of social or business networks
- A target based sales management role
- A human resources based role
- A new start opportunity
- A project management role

Weaknesses

- Nervous when presenting
- Easily led
- Impulsive
- Get bored easily
- Suffer fools badly
- Hate to be seen to make a mistake
- Lack of confidence
- Lack of commercial bandwidth

Threats

- My ideas may not always be heard
- My opinions are not always sought or recognized
- Doesn't see the bigger picture
- Lacks attention to detail
- Disregards the views of others
- Won't take risks
- Seen as negative and pessimistic
- Naive and inexperienced

The importance of prioritising the opportunities and threats is that it encourages you to identify those on which you should concentrate first. It is equally important not to try and address everything at once. Select one or two strengths to reinforce and one or two weaknesses to work on. This will make the task more manageable and ensure that you make steady and effective progress as you work through the list over time.

There are a great many Self Perception Inventory tools available to us. Many of them are easily accessible and simple to complete. Some are behavioural, such as Belbin and some are more psychometrically based, such as Myers-Briggs, TalentQ Dimensions personality questionnaire and Insights. I would strongly urge you to complete at least one, if not two or three of them. I believe that they provide a fascinating insight into yourself, which, although subjectively based, provides another tool in your armoury.

I must admit to a degree of cynicism the first time that I completed one. I didn't really believe that the output based upon answering a few straightforward questions would be of any great value. How wrong I was. Whether or not you agree with the 'pigeon-hole' that you are put into is not the point. What I found to be of immense help was the questions that the output made me ask of myself. It was like having an inner coach, a voice in your head that made you question yourself and prove things to yourself. It provided me with provocation and made me consider things from an alternative perspective, the "on the other hand" if you like.

The results from the analysis that I completed became a major building block of my own self-awareness. What I found of particular use were the negative or developmental areas associated with my 'stereotype'. Once I had got over my "Well, that doesn't apply to me" arrogance, it encouraged me to ask myself what action I needed to take do in order to overcome the less welcome characteristics common in my 'psyche'.

For the record, my Belbin outcome varies slightly each time I complete the questionnaire, usually because my business or personal focus has shifted slightly. However, I consistently score very high on Shaper and Coordinator and always very low on Team Worker.

Shapers are task-focused leaders who abound in nervous energy, have a high motivation to achieve and for whom winning is the name of the game. The shaper is committed to achieving and will 'shape' others into accomplishing the aims of the team. He or she will challenge, argue or disagree and will display aggression in the pursuit of goal achievement.

Coordinators often become the default chairperson of a team, stepping back to see the big picture. Coordinators are confident, stable and mature and because they recognise abilities in others, they are very good at delegating tasks to the right person for the job. The Coordinator clarifies decisions, helping everyone else focus on their tasks. Coordinators are sometimes perceived to be manipulative, and will tend to delegate all work, leaving nothing but the delegating for them to do.

Team Workers are diplomats and good listeners. They help to smooth over conflicts and are less confrontational than others.

My consistently low score in this behavioural type or team role raises the provocation that these attributes may not be ones that come to me too naturally. In fact they are in conflict with some of the attributes that do manifest themselves in me more readily. Therefore there is a need for me to take action to proactively work on developing these qualities if they are important in what I do.

My Myers-Briggs Type Indicator is ESTP; which means that I prefer extraversion to introversion, sensing preferred to intuition, thinking preferred to feeling and perceiving preferred to judging. According to Myers-Briggs ESTP's are hands-on learners who live in the moment, seeking the best in life, wanting to share it with their friends. The ESTP is open to situations, able to improvise to bring about desired results. They are active people who want to solve their problems rather than simply discuss them.

According to the psychologist David Keirsey, ESTP's, or "Promoter Artisans", are the most adept among the types at manipulating other people. Promoting is the art of manoeuvring others to one's position. Concrete in speech and utilitarian in action, they are smooth operators. The ESTP knows everyone who matters and everything there is to do because they are very resourceful, always knowing where the fun and action is. They like to indulge themselves in the finer things in life and to bring other people with them. Their goal in life is to sell themselves and their ideas to others. Dramatic and debonair, they are gifted at earning others' confidence.

Insights Discovery profile describes me as an 'Inspiring Motivator' consciously and a 'Directing Motivator' less consciously. It describes me as imaginative, innovative and an improviser. It goes on to say that I am permanently positive, persuasive and completely committed. All great stuff which, of course, I am in complete agreement with.

But then comes the kicker. The flip side of the coin. I can be disorganised and undisciplined. I take criticism of my work personally, I tend to exaggerate, can sometimes be over optimistic and, because I like new challenges, can jump, seemingly randomly from task to task.

What intrigues me is how consistent the outcomes are, from three distinctly different tools. There can be no smoke without fire and it is this degree of consistency that encouraged me to take the outcomes more seriously and do something about them.

Whilst the initial definitions make for enjoyable reading, there are less savoury undertones that consistently rise to the surface regarding arrogance, aggressiveness, manipulating people and situations, over indulgence and lack of attention to detail. Things that I initially chose to ignore (rather arrogantly) but eventually came to try and address as I could see that they were the negative sides to my character that I needed to proactively do something about.

There is another significant benefit to be gained from completing any form of self awareness analysis. The questionnaires that you complete in order to generate your results demand that you be selective in your choices. They are either normative or Likert (where you rank the options in order of preference) or they are ipsative (where you are forced to make a choice between options) or a mixture of both. By definition you are actively *not* choosing certain options by deliberately selecting others. As your choices are collated the output leans you towards one 'type' or another and as a result away from the other types available in the test results. The inevitable consequence of classifying us one way or another is that we are less like the other types available to us. What this should highlight to us is that there are other people who do fall into the other categories. I have found that a significant benefit of these tests is that they heighten my awareness of differences between people and the fact that I need to adapt my style with these people in order to interact with them more effectively.

Take a look at the model below and intuitively place yourself in one of the quadrants based upon how you perceive yourself.

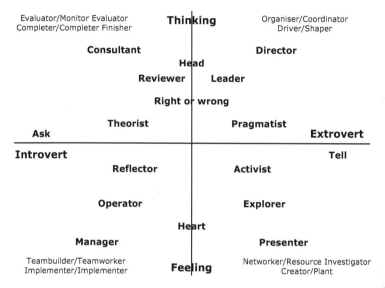

Now try to place other people that you know into the alternative quadrants to highlight the differing styles and attitudes that they have. Once you become more conscious of that individual's traits and characteristics you can modify the style that you use with them in order to be more effective and appealing to them.

I work with many individuals on the development of their management and leadership style, their communication techniques and their Personal Brand Essence. I always ask them to complete a Personal Development Questionnaire before we meet for the first time. The questionnaire asks some obvious, but nonetheless difficult, questions that require the respondent to begin thinking in a different way. I have documented the questionnaire below and recommend that you make a record of your own answers to add to your personal

SWOT, the outcome of any Self Perception Inventories that you have completed and the work that you did in Chapter 3 on defining the components of your own Personal Brand Essence.

Personal

What do you do?

What are your real motivators?

What are your personal goals in life?

What challenges you?

What is unique and differentiating about you?

How would you define your personal style?

How would you define your behaviours?

What are your values?

How would you define your personal proposition?

How would you define your Personal Brand Essence?

Business

What are your targets?

What are your objectives?

How will you achieve your targets and objectives?

What milestones and measures have you set yourself?

How do you make a difference?

What will you become famous for?

Which areas would you like to develop?

Who are your target audiences?

What are your communication messages to those audiences?

How do you want your colleagues to deal with you?

It is essential that feedback forms part of your personal awareness analysis. It would be foolhardy to assume that we are good at something if we were unable to evidence it. It would be pointless to work on developing an area of weakness if we were unable to ascertain that the action that we had taken had not addressed it.

I believe that it is vital that we start with ourselves when we are attempting to identify who we are and what we stand for. It is the natural place to start, with the obvious question being 'Who am I?' Most organisations also build their brand from the inside out. They quite rightly focus upon their people, their products, their culture and their heritage before turning to their customers and seeking a way of communicating their brand and the benefits that it brings in an attractive way.

However, the best organisations also adopt an outside in approach. They find out what their customers' perceptions are and how they are influenced by the behaviours that they see from the company and the performance of its products and services. This should not be any different for us at a personal level. We need to be clear about who we think we are but we also need to test and validate the authenticity of our conclusions with our 'customers'. We need to adopt an outside in approach as well.

360 degree feedback is an excellent methodology for ensuring that we measure and monitor our performance and receive objective feedback that is both qualitative and quantitative. 360 degree feedback is so called because it puts you at the centre of a circle of people providing you with feedback. The people in your feedback circle should include someone senior to yourself, peers and subordinates as well as trusted confidants, mentors and friends. Ideally, you should have six to eight people in the circle as this forces you to choose who is included within it carefully as well as keeping the feedback loop tight and manageable.

Initially, ask your feedback circle for their opinions on your strengths and weaknesses and for evidence and examples to support their comments. Then, once every six months or so, ask them to comment on the progress that they have noticed as a result of the action that you have taken to hone your strengths and address your weaknesses. This feedback should be written rather than verbal as it will encourage your circle to provide you with considered opinions and allow you to reflect upon what they have actually said rather than what you think they meant.

It is important not to issue your feedback questionnaire to your feedback circle too often. Firstly, it allows you time, between surveys, to modify and change your behaviours and for the results to be noticed. Secondly, it does not become too onerous a task for your feedback circle to complete. In the same spirit, make sure that the questions on which you are seeking feedback are limited to between six and ten. This will compel you to be selective about your questions and will not deter your circle from completing the questionnaire by issuing them with the equivalent of *War and Peace*.

The questions that you ask need to be very relevant to the priority strengths and weaknesses that you are currently working on. Ask for evidentiary comment to obtain the qualitative input and a mark out of 10 to arrive at the quantitative score. Ask the same questions of each of your respondents and compare and contrast their answers to arrive at an overall commentary and performance indicator. Don't be tempted to disregard what you may see as over-critical feedback. This is often the most telling of the observations that you receive. As well as asking your circle to provide comment, also ask them to offer some suggestions as this will help you to evolve and improve your own personal action plan. Change and refine your questions as the process continues and as you look for feedback on new strengths and weaknesses that you are concentrating on.

Your personal awareness analysis should contain all four of the elements that I have outlined above. A personal SWOT, at least one Personal Perception Inventory, a completed personal development questionnaire and a 360 degree feedback circle.

You will have an enhanced view of yourself as a result of completing this analysis. Your own views will be tempered by those of others providing you with greater objectivity and balance. You will have a much better grasp of where to start and the direction that you need to take. Of what is possible for you to achieve.

EXAMPLE

360 Degree Feedback Questionnaire

What do I do well?

What could I do better?

How would you rate my overall attitude out of 10? ☐
What could I do to improve my overall attitude?

How would you rate my personal image out of 10? ☐
What could I do to improve my personal image?

How would you rate my style with people out of 10? ☐
What could I do to improve my people style?

How would you rate my communication skills out of 10? ☐
What could I do to improve my communication skills?

If I should do one thing differently to be more consistent with my Personal Brand Essence and the perceptions that I am trying to create what would that be?

So What?

- Before we can improve ourselves we have to understand ourselves. We need to know where to start from and where to focus our energies.

- There are a number of ways that we can improve upon our own personal awareness:

  1. Personal SWOT
  2. Pscychometric tests
  3. Self Perception Inventories
  4. Personal Development Questionnaire
  5. 360 degree feedback

5

The rules of successful personal development

"It's never too late to be what we might have been."
From Middlemarch by George Eliot

There are no great secrets to personal development. In fact, one of the great problems that people face is that they know they should be doing something but never quite get around to it.

In my experience one of the most fulfilling things that you can do is to spend some time on developing yourself. My suggestion would be that you put some time aside every month in your diary and make a commitment to yourself that you will keep the appointment that you have made with yourself. Even an hour a week will give you six days more than most of us currently dedicate to the responsibility in the course of a year. Over the course of time, the improvement in your performance, your success both at home and at work and the achievement of your personal goals will become more than evident.

I have developed a set of rules that I try to abide by myself. They have helped me to feel more in control of my own personal development and encouraged me to take a more proactive approach to improving myself over the years.

Rule 1. Start with you

Once you have made the commitment to spend some time on yourself it helps to have a plan of campaign. I would counsel you to start with yourself. Self awareness is 90% of the answer; the remaining 10% is doing something about it. If you know you have a challenge then you can start to do something about it. Know yourself. Understand what makes you, you. Understand what is important to you and identify your values. Be clear in your own mind of your capabilities and your limitations. Ask yourself what you enjoy and what you dislike, both at work and at home. Recognise the things that challenge you and motivate you. The work that you did in the previous chapter will have given you many of the answers to these provocations.

Rule 2. Define and develop your Personal Brand Essence

Every time you leave the house you are judged, usually sub consciously, by people. How you dress, how you talk, the things that you say, the way that you behave, all help to form peoples' opinion of you. Become more conscious of your personal brand. Ask yourself what you stand for and how those values and principles manifest themselves in your behaviour, your attitudes and your performance. You will have a good feel for your brand now and we explore how you take the components that you identified in Chapter 3 and turn them into your own Personal Brand Essence definition in Chapter 10.

Rule 3. Make a difference

The most successful people in life usually have a 'big idea', something that they become famous for. Now it may not be as ground-breaking as discovering penicillin, or inventing the Internet but work on developing things that you are known for. The things that will become your vehicles in life, your unique contribution. Build your reputation. We will examine this in more detail in Chapter 9.

Rule 4. Live and have fun

Life is too short, so the saying goes and whilst you probably can't live every day as though it were your last, you should at the very least enjoy yourself. Get out of your comfort zone as often as you can, test yourself, take considered risks and frighten yourself every once in a while. Personal performance is enhanced dramatically through personal experiences and the anchors that they create.

It is critical that we are happy at home, that we love our partner, our friends and our house because that is why we work, in order to earn the money that enables us to lead the life that we wish to lead.

We have to do a job that excites us, that interests us and that we enjoy. We have to be suited to it and the personal SWOT that you completed in Chapter 4 will have given you an indication of the sort of role that could suit you at work. If you don't like your job you have to do something about it. You have to find the role that suits your skills and appeals to you. You may not get out of bed every morning punching the air with delight at the thought of going to work but you have to be happy, fulfilled and excited by it. If not, do something about it.

Rule 5. Take action

Inertia is the greatest enemy of anyone embarking on personal development. Once you have taken the time to decide to do something you must see it through to completion. Planning when you are going to take action enables you to break down the task and becomes positively habit forming. Mark time to take action in your diary and get accustomed to taking time out to develop yourself on a frequent and regular basis.

Rule 6. Focus

One of the great benefits of consciously working out what you should be doing is that it allows you to stop doing irrelevant and unproductive things. Not only does this in itself save you time, time that you can employ on self improvement, but it also allows you to mentally turn the volume down on the wall of noise that surrounds all of us and focus on achieving your personal objectives and goals.

Rule 7. Mentor and be mentored

Mentoring is one of the most powerful tools in an individual's developmental armoury. The benefits from talking things through, ideally with someone who can furnish you with an objective view are manifold. I have found that I have gained even more from mentoring than I have from being mentored and I would strongly suggest that you do both. It is one of the most effective ways of growing your commercial and personal bandwidth, which we look at it more detail in Chapter 13.

Rule 8. Never stop learning

We must constantly seek ways in which to improve ourselves. Personal development is an iterative process, the task is never complete, you just move from one milestone to another. As your career progresses, so will the relevance and importance of new skills, attitudes and knowledge, as a result your personal development plan needs to evolve with you.

Developing and practicing skills, coupled with the right attitude, leads to improved confidence and greater self-belief. It is what enables us to play in the performance zone and we will explore some of the things that can be done in more detail in Chapter 15.

Rule 9. Realise your potential

Not everyone wants to be a high flying Chief Executive. Individual aspirations and ambitions are, quite rightly, tailored by the person themselves. As we will find in the next chapter, if we apply ourselves to the task we can, with a little thought and time, define quite clearly what it is that we want to achieve both at home and at work. The only thing that limits us is our imagination. The barriers that we perceive can be overcome with the right determination and application. No one can knock your ambitions, provided they are well thought through, because they are yours. The responsibility that you have is to ensure that you own them and that you deliver upon them, whether they be great or small. Determining the path that we need to take in order to achieve our dreams is the important thing, knowing where to start. The first step on the journey is the hardest because it dictates the direction that we will take.

Rule 10. Never underestimate what you can achieve

Over the years I have been astounded by the giant leaps in personal competence and ability that people who are determined enough can make. The confidence that they get from achieving their goals empowers them and propels them forward to the next challenge that they have set for themselves.

I have witnessed this year after year at the *bssa* Oxford Summer School which is held at Keble College in Oxford. Young, bright delegates from all manner of retailers leave the school inspired to do something with their careers, to set themselves some milestones and to take personal ownership for delivering them. This is no different from watching a child grow and learn through practise and experience or seeing a teenage terror flourish and develop as they rise through the ranks at work. Success breeds success and small steps ultimately lead to great distances being covered. Think back to your very first day at work and compare yourself now with that young, inexperienced memory. All of us have made great strides as individuals as we have matured, mostly sub-consciously, without really thinking about it or having a plan. Think about what you have already achieved in your life, both personally and professionally and ask yourself how much of it was planned and predetermined by yourself. How much more quickly would you have achieved it if you had proactively set out to do so? How much more could you have achieved? How much more can you still yet achieve?

So What?

There are 10 rules for successful personal development:

Rule 1. **Start with you.**

Rule 2. **Define your Personal Brand Essence.**

Rule 3. **Make a difference.**

Rule 4. **Live and have fun.**

Rule 5. **Take action.**

Rule 6. **Focus.**

Rule 7. **Mentor and be mentored.**

Rule 8. **Never stop learning.**

Rule 9. **Realise your potential.**

Rule 10. **Never underestimate what you can achieve.**

6

Personal Life Plan

"You've never seen the Alhambra? Or the walls of Toledo? Or Venice? Ayers Rock. Machu Pichu. They are there waiting for you. The places other people have been. Now it's your turn."
Pam Brown

When was the first time that you realised you were going to die? That you were not immortal? For many of us it was the death of a loved grandparent or perhaps the death of a family pet. For others it may have been a near death experience in our early years. The fact is that, as Benjamin Franklin pointed out, it is one of the few certainties in life.

Tchaikovsky, the Russian composer, once mused "How short life is! How much I have still to do, to think and to say! We keep putting things off and meanwhile death lurks round the corner".

What I found quite scary is that when I finally started to put together my own Personal Life Plan, a realisation dawned upon me that I didn't have a whole heap of time left. I realised that at 35 years of age that I was already half way through my allotted time and that I hadn't done any of the things that I really wanted to do. In fact I wasn't even certain of what those things were!

Mark Twain wrote that "Twenty years from now you will be more disappointed by the things that you didn't do than by the ones you did do. Explore. Dream. Discover."

I just knew that the clock was ticking and that I needed to have a plan. I needed to explore, dream and discover. I needed to more fully understand what motivated me, what I wanted to achieve and what my legacy was going to be.

I have a real issue with Personal Development Plans. On the whole they are a pointless exercise, often completed once a year at an annual performance review and consigned to a dusty shelf or the bottom of a filing cabinet. My argument is that they are usually the last thing that is discussed at an appraisal or a performance review and are often completed with a few feeble words along the lines of a training course that should be attended or meeting with someone that should be arranged. They rarely have context or relevance and are therefore never referred back to, well, not until the following year's appraisal anyway.

Personal Development Plans have to be live documents. They have to evolve with the individual as he or she develops. They need to be specific and to enable something to happen. We will look at what I believe is a more effective form of Personal Development Plan in the next chapter, but before we can create one we need to think about our Personal Life Plan first. We work to live, not live to work. Work is an enabler. It provides us with the income that enables us to do the things that we really want to in life. There is no point in developing oneself unless the outcome enables us to achieve what is important to us and this is where the process begins, by identifying the things that are really essential to us.

The Personal Life Plan consists of four elements. Goals, time, age and money. It is designed to encourage you to identify the things that you want to do in life, put a time frame around when you will accomplish them, give you a reality check as to how old you will be when you attain each one and how much money you will need to have in order to enable them to happen. I have found that using a simple spreadsheet allows you to condense your thoughts into a single document and relate each of the headings to each goal. The document is something that you can easily carry around with you, refer to and enhance as frequently as you wish. It becomes a tool and an aide memoire rather than a chore.

Goals

Begin by listing all of your personal life goals, your aims and your aspirations. All of the things that you want to achieve before you die. Think about all of the things that are personally significant to you. Family, friends and your work. Possessions, holidays and your home. Health, wealth and your retirement.

It almost goes without saying that your own personal life goals are unique and individual to you. However, what I want to do is provide you with an example of what a set of life goals could look like, in order to illustrate how the Personal Life Plan builds up around those goals. Our own goals will, of course, be very specific to us. They will be driven by our age, by our current circumstances, by what we have already achieved and by what we now realise is unrealistic or simply not possible. Referring back to the personal awareness analysis that you completed in Chapter 4 will help you to create your own list of your life goals.

The example below is based upon the sort of things that may be stereotypically included in the list of a twenty year old just starting work and living at home with their parents. Clearly it is not an exhaustive list and I have deliberately tried to make it generic in order not to lead you but to help to stimulate your thought process.

1. Buy a car
2. Move into my first home
3. Set up home
4. Fortnight abroad every year
5. Get married
6. Have my first child
7. Upsize to a semi-detached house in a better area
8. Upgrade the car
9. Have my second child
10. Weekends in European capital cities
11. First child starts school
12. Second child starts school
13. Join a golf club
14. Upsize to a detached house in a better area
15. Children go to university

16. Children get married
17. Live and work abroad
18. Travel the world
19. Buy a property abroad
20. Retire

Time

Once you are satisfied that you have included all of your goals we need to provide some sort of time bound framework against which to work. Try and put them in some sort of chronological order. If they were a series of milestones along the path you have chosen to take, in which order will they appear? What is the sequence in which they will come into view? Is the accomplishment of one dependent upon the realisation of another? Realistically, how long will it take to achieve each of the shorter term goals? What is your self-imposed timeframe for the longer term goals?

1. Buy a car
   This year.

2. Move into my first home
   This year.

3. Set up home
   Over the next couple of years.

4. Fortnight abroad every year
   In 3 years time.

5. Get married
   In about 5 years time.

6. Have my first child
   In about 7 years time.

7. Upsize to a semi-detached house in a better area
   In about 8 years time.

8. Upgrade the car
    In about 9 years time.

9. Have my second child
    A couple of years after the first.

10. Weekends in European capital cities
    In about 10 years time.

11. First child starts school
    When they are five.

12. Second child starts school
    When they are five.

13. Join a golf club
    Once I'm in my thirties.

14. Upsize to a detached house in a better area
    Before I get to forty.

15. Children go to university
    When they are 18.

16. Children get married
    When they are in their twenties.

17. Live and work abroad
    Before I get to fifty.

18. Travel around the world
    On my fiftieth birthday.

19. Buy a property abroad
    Before I retire.

20. Retire
    Before I get to sixty.

Age

Now, this is the slightly scary bit, especially if, like me, you are not twenty and living with Mum and Dad when you do this for the first time. You may want to remove all pills and sharp objects from the room before starting. Note your current age and then roll the clock forward and record the age you will be when you pass each milestone. One of the great benefits of this part of the Personal Life Plan is that it forces you to ask some very pertinent questions of yourself. It forces you to be realistic and to reprioritise your list. It can sometimes even make you remove things from the list because it will just not be feasible to achieve them in the time you have left. It provides you with clarity and encourages you to focus and redouble your efforts to achieve want you want to achieve with greater urgency and determination.

1. Buy a car
    This year.
    Age 20.

2. Move into my first home
    This year.
    Age 20.

3. Set up home
    Over the next couple of years.
    Age 21.

4. Fortnight abroad every year
    In 3 years time.
    Age 23.

5. Get married
    In about 5 years time.
    Age 25.

6. Have my first child
    In about 7 years time.
    Age 27.

7. Upsize to a semi-detached house in a better area
    In about 8 years time.
    Age 28.

8. Upgrade the car
    In about 9 years time.
    Age 29.

9. Have my second child
    A couple of years after the first.
    Age 29.

10. Weekends in European capital cities
    In about 10 years time.
    Age 30.

11. First child starts school
    When they are five.
    Age 32.

12. Second child starts school
    When they are five.
    Age 34.

13. Join a golf club
    Once I'm in my thirties.
    Age 36.

14. Upsize to a detached house in a better area
    Before I get to forty.
    Age 38.

15. Children go to university
    When they are 18.
    Age 45.

16. Children get married
    When they are in their twenties.
    Age 47.

17. Live and work abroad
    Before I get to fifty.
    Age 48.

18. Travel around the world
    On my fiftieth birthday.
    Age 50.

19. Buy a property abroad
    Before I retire.
    Age 53.

20. Retire
    Before I get to sixty.
    Age 55.

Money

I appreciate that not all of the goals that you have identified will be materialistic. However, be careful that the goals you have set for yourself are not too altruistic or vague. To be happy is a natural thing to include in your list but you need to get far deeper into what you mean by happiness. What makes you happy is represented by a series of things that collectively add up to happiness in your eyes. Many of these things are indeed materialistic and therefore have a cost or an earnings requirement associated with them.

Many people will identify voluntary or charitable work, gap years or spiritual fulfilment in their list of personal goals. Whilst these may not have a monetary cost directly associated with them they will necessitate a sound financial footing to underpin the achievement of them. So, identify the literal or enabling costs associated with each goal and record the estimated earnings requirement (in today's money) that will needed to fulfil it.

1. Buy a car
   This year.
   Age 20.
   Current salary £15,000.

2. Move into my first home
    This year.
    Age 20.
    Required salary £18,000.

3. Set up home
    Over the next couple of years.
    Age 21.
    Required salary £18,000.

4. Fortnight abroad every year
    In 3 years time.
    Age 23.
    Required salary £20,000.

5. Get married
    In about 5 years time.
    Age 25.
    Required salary £25,000.

6. Have my first child
    In about 7 years time.
    Age 27.
    Required salary £28,000.

7. Upsize to a semi-detached house in a better area
    In about 8 years time.
    Age 28.
    Required salary £30,000.

8. Upgrade the car
    In about 9 years time.
    Age 29.
    Required salary £30,000.

9. Have my second child
    A couple of years after the first.
    Age 29.
    Required salary £30,000.

10. Weekends in European capital cities
    In about 10 years time.
    Age 30.
    Required salary £33,000.

11. First child starts school
    When they are five.
    Age 32.
    Required salary £35,000.

12. Second child starts school
    When they are five.
    Age 34.
    Required salary £38,000.

13. Join a golf club
    Once I'm in my thirties.
    Age 36.
    Required salary £40,000.

14. Upsize to a detached house in a better area
    Before I get to forty.
    Age 38.
    Required salary £45,000.

15. Children go to university
    When they are 18.
    Age 45.
    Required salary £50,000.

16. Children get married
    When they are in their twenties.
    Age 47.
    Required salary £55,000.

17. Live and work abroad
    Before I get to fifty.
    Age 48.
    Required salary £60,000.

18. Travel around the world
    On my fiftieth birthday.
    Age 50.
    Required salary £65,000.

19. Buy a property abroad
    Before I retire.
    Age 53.
    Required salary £65,000.

20. Retire
    Before I get to sixty.
    Age 55.
    Reqired salary £70,000.

Recorded on a spread sheet, the example that I have outlined above may look something like this. . .

What are your goals in life?	When will you achieve them?	What will it cost?
Personal relationships	How old are you now?	How much do you earn now?
Friends and family	How long will each one take?	How much is needed for each goal?
House and home	How old will you be then?	Can you earn that amount?
Holidays and travel	Are your timescales realistic?	Are your timescales realistic?
Professional achievement	What is your target retirement age?	Should you re-prioritise?
Personal possessions	What are your key priorities?	What are your key priorities?
Retirement	Does anything need to go?	Does anything need to go?

GOALS	YEAR	AGE	REQUIRED SALARY
Buy a car	2005	20	£15,000
Move into my first home	2005	20	£18,000
Set up home	2006	21	£18,000
Fortnight abroad every year	2008	23	£20,000
Get married	2010	25	£25,000
Have my first child	2013	28	£28,000
Up size to a semi detached house	2013	28	£30,000
Upgrade the car	2014	29	£30,000
Have my second child	2014	29	£30,000
Weekends in European capital cities	2015	30	£33,000
First child starts school	2017	32	£35,000
Second child starts school	2019	34	£38,000
Join a golf club	2021	36	£40,000
Up size to a detached house	2023	38	£45,000
Children go to university	2030	45	£50,000
Children get married	2032	47	£55,000
Live and work abroad	2033	48	£60,000
Travel around the world	2035	50	£65,000
Buy a property abroad	2038	53	£65,000
Retire	2040	55	£70,000

I know from personal experience that things happen to us as we travel along the path. Relationships fail, opportunities that we had not previously considered materialise, the unexpected occurs as fate plays its part. These changes in circumstance can often bring new influences to bear on us and as a result, alter the priorities and content of our Personal Life Plan. So be it. If we have a plan then at least we can modify it to take them into account. It is too easy not to make a plan because we know that there will be alterations. The plan helps to provide focus. It enables us to take considered, targeted and measurable action. It enables us to create a personal development plan that is relevant, impactful and that we are in control of.

So What?

- Work is a means to an end. We go to work to make money to spend on delivering and achieving our personal life goals, the things that are important to us.

- To maximise our chances of delivering these goals we need to create an effective Personal Life Plan which consists of the following elements:

    1. What are our personal life goals?
    2. When do we want to achieve them by?
    3. How old will we be when we achieve them?
    4. How much money will they cost to achieve?

7

Personal Development Plan

"If now is not the time to act, when will it be?"
Hillel

A friend of mine is a plasterer. He is a fine plasterer. A tradesman. He knows exactly how to do what he does, he has perfected his art over many years and he is very good at it. He wakes at 6am every morning, knocks up his mix and puts his skills to work. Every day. That's what he does.

He once asked me a very good question. He asked me "What do you do?" There was nothing Machiavellian in his question, he wasn't trying to trick me or catch me out, it was asked out of genuine interest. What I found difficult was answering it as succinctly as he described what he did for a living. It set off a train of thought in my mind that was to ultimately lead to the creation of my own personal development plan.

Things happened to me. I was lucky because others saw something in me that I had not recognised myself. They saw potential and opportunity came my way as a result. In many ways I was unconsciously competent and my career progressed, not due to some grand plan but more by chance and circumstance. It was not until my mid-thirties that the realisation dawned upon me that I could, no; should, be proactive in my own development. I needed to take control of the direction that I was heading in. I needed to be more responsible for my actions and the decisions that I made about my career. I needed to write my grand plan.

If you live in a house with a garden, or occasionally take a walk in a park on a bright autumnal day, you will notice that when the leaves have fallen from the trees the breeze tends to tidy the leaves. Over the course of a few days most of the leaves will form a pile in the corner of the driveway or against a fence in the park. They will end up where the breeze has chosen to put them. Just now and then a rogue leaf will refuse to conform and takes flight in a different direction, almost wilfully resisting the gust that has accounted for its contemporaries.

I was one of the leaves in the pile. Yes, I had been blown there by the buffeting that we are all susceptible to, but I did not resist. I did not even think about taking a different course of action. I allowed fate to dictate where I landed. My friend's question prompted many more. Not just; what do you do, but; why do you do it and what else could you do? It provoked me to take hold of the tiller and set a course rather than just drift on the current.

Why do we go to work? Partly because we are conditioned to do so, partly because we have a responsibility to do so and partly because we have a desire to do so. It is a way of giving something back, particularly for those who are driven by a vocation, but ultimately it is to earn an income. I would contend that even if we won several million on the lottery we would still work. Not because we had to but because we wanted to. We may work in the community or become actively involved with our favourite charity or establish our own business. We would do something more than idle our lives away counting the money. We would put the money to work to explore, to fulfil our dreams and discover more about ourselves.

Once we know what we want, why we want it and what we need in order to achieve it, we can create our Personal Development Plan. We can individually tailor the plan to address the skills that we need to develop in order to secure the positions that will pay us the salary that will enable us to fund the things that really matter to us. The delivery of our goals.

As the Personal Life Plan consists of four elements, so does the Personal Development Plan. Job, skills, gaps and action. The Personal Development Plan is designed to build upon the content that you created when completing your Personal Life Plan in the previous chapter. If you chose to use a spreadsheet to capture your Personal Life Plan, you can simply add four additional columns in which to record your Personal Development Plan. The first stage is to identify the type of job that you will need to do in order to generate the income that you need to fund each of the goals that you have set for yourself. The skills section builds upon the personal SWOT analysis that you completed in Chapter 4. The gaps element identifies the skills that you need to develop in order to progress to the next level at work. The final stage is designed to provide you with a time-bound framework of the action that you need to take in order to close that skills gap in time to gain the promotion that will deliver the increased income required to accomplish your next set of goals.

Job

The first part of this is pretty straightforward. Answer the question; what do you do? Note here your current job and the salary that it pays. The second part is a little more challenging. Ask yourself the following questions and make a note of your answers. Do you enjoy it? Why? Does the job interest you? Is it suited to your likes and dislikes? Does the salary enable you to fund all of the things that you want to achieve in the short term? Does it make use of all of your skills? Does it offer you the opportunity to grow with your potential?

Depending upon the answers to these provocations you may need to take some dramatic steps. You may decide that you are not doing the job that is most suited to your skills or your interests. It may not offer you the growth potential that you now realise you need to have. If this is the case, do something about it. Take some action. Seek out employment that you will enjoy and that plays to your strengths and your desires. Hopefully, however, you will already be doing a job that you enjoy and that offers you the opportunities that you seek for the future. Now you can concentrate on developing your skills and your personal brand to ensure that your career really starts to take off.

Using the worked example from the previous chapter we can see that our twenty year old needs to grow their salary by around £5,000 over the next three years in order to be able to afford to secure their first home, furnish it and pay for a good holiday every year. It is conceivable that pay reviews over the succeeding three years will grow their salary from £15,000 to £20,000 but unlikely. What is more likely is that a promotion will be required in order to generate the required step change in income.

Skills

Be very clear about what you are good at and be able to evidence it and prove it to anyone who may have a legitimate interest. You will have identified some weaknesses when completing your personal SWOT analysis. The issue is not that you have weaknesses, after all, no one is perfect. More relevantly you can decide upon which of your weaknesses is a potential drawback to your career aspirations and focus on addressing those. You can actively choose not to take action on some of them because they are less relevant and damaging to your prospects than the others.

Many positions are filled within organisations by candidates who are able to evidence that they possess the core competencies required to meet the demands of the role. These evidence based interviewing techniques are rightly becoming more commonplace and we need to prepare for them accordingly.

Create a personal skills list and record it here. You are providing the evidence that your core competencies are fit for purpose in the context of your current role. Your current skills list needs to be detailed and supported with good examples of how you have developed and used each skill, previously or currently. You will undoubtedly have identified other skills, over and above those needed to meet the requirements of the job that you currently do. Some of these skills may well be more relevant to the position above you in the organisation. They could lend themselves to you being able to demonstrate that you have the core competencies required to achieve promotion to that next level of the business.

Gap

The chances are of course, that whilst you may have some of what it takes to do the next job, you will probably have some skills gaps as well. Take a look around the business that you work for. Most companies are multifaceted. They offer careers in sales, marketing, human resources, finance, production and many other areas. Choose the one that is best suited to you and identify the different levels and grades that sit within that discipline. Hunt down the job descriptions and pay scales for each of those grades and discover what each of those roles entails from a skills and experience perspective.

Now compare them to your current role and your own skills and experiences. Note here the disparity between your current skills level and the level required and expected for the more senior role. You have now specified your skills and experience variance and have a clear indication of the existing skills that you need to hone and of the new skills that you need to develop.

Going back to our twenty year old, we could list the skills that they may currently possess in order to perform at the level required to justify their £15,000 salary. Let's call those essential skills A, B, C, D and E. Based upon our research, we would also be able to identify the skills required of someone in the more senior position earning £20,000. Let's call those essential skills C, D, E, F, G and H. The skills gap that they need to bridge in order to gain the promotion they desire is F, G and H. They would almost certainly also need to develop the existing skills of C, D and E too as whilst they are the same skills they will probably need to be used in a slightly different way.

Action

Finally, we need to note the action that we need to take in order to address the skills gap that we have acknowledged. This action should be very specific, with detailed timescales and with specific outcomes associated with each of them. It could entail spending some time covering for the more senior individual whilst they are away on holiday. It could involve asking to have a task usually completed by the more senior individual delegated to you on a permanent basis. It could include shadowing an individual already in the more senior position for a period of time to gain exposure to the demands of the job. And, yes, it may well require going on a course or attending a meeting with someone who can help you with the specific requirement. But whatever the action is, it will be targeted, it will be specific and it will be measurable. When the day comes that you are asked to evidence the skill at a promotion board you will be able to do so, with confidence. What is more, you will be able to demonstrate that it wasn't just by chance, it was part of a well thought through plan. It was premeditated and evidenced on the next steps contained in your annual performance review.

And so the process continues throughout the Personal Life Plan. What job do I need to do next to provide me with the income required to fund the associated goals? What skills do I currently possess that fit the requirements of that job? What are my skills gaps and what do I need to do in order to be able demonstrate to my employer that I have addressed those gaps?

I agree that you cannot have your entire career mapped out before you at the age of twenty. However, what you can decide upon is a route, a general direction in which you will head. You may not be able to anticipate every twist and turn in the road but you do know that your general direction should be, say, North and that you can ignore landmarks and signposts that suggest that you should be tempted to head East or West, or worse still, South. It minimises the distractions that we all encounter on the journey and helps us to get where we are heading more effectively and with greater efficiency.

Many people hold the view that as your career progresses, the heights that you scale are often not as a result of what you know but are dictated by who you know. Personal networks are critically important and we will explore these in more detail in Chapter 13. Role models, mentors and sponsors all play a vital part in our careers but in my experience, once you have attained a certain level within an organisation it is the people with vision and the ideas to support that vision who progress. Attitude rather than skill on its own, ultimately wins the day. We need to answer the question that is posed in Chapter 9. What will you be famous for?

What are your current skills?	What is the next step?	Identify your skills gap	What are you going to do?
What are you good at?	Identify other roles in the business	List you current skills	Prioritise your activity
What evidence do you have?	What would you enjoy?	List the skills you still require	Set SMART objectives
What do you need to be better at?	What would you be good at?	List the skills you will require	Identify role models
Why would that be beneficial?	What do the roles entail?	Highlight the matches	Target influential people
What are you best at?	What skills will you need?	Prioritise the gaps	Search for mentors
What would you do if you could do anything you wanted to?	Who are the influencers?		Ask for sponsors
	How will you influence them?		Build a personal 360 network

SKILLS	ROLES	GAPS	ACTION

So What?

- Personal Development Plans are, in the main, a waste of time. This is because they are not focussed in the right way.

- An effective Personal Development Plan must focus on the skills that we need to develop in order obtain the job that will earn us the income that we need in order to deliver the personal life goals that we have set for ourselves.

- Our Personal Development Plan should contain the following elements:
  1. The work that motivates us and that we enjoy doing.
  2. The skills that we need to secure that work.
  3. The gap between our existing skills and those required.
  4. The specific action that we will take to close the gap.

Personal Life Plan and Personal Development Plan

PLP	Life Goals	Year	Age	Finances	PDP	Job	Skills	Gaps	Action	Network	Role Models	Mentors	Sponsors
	Record here the personal life goals that you have set for yourself. List them in chronological order. Consider family, children, partner, home, travel, possessions, retirement etc.	Record here the target year by which you hope to have achieved your personal life goal.	Record here the age that you will be in the year that you aim to achieve your personal life goal.	Record here the annual income that you will require in order to pay for the realisation of your personal life goal.		Identify the kind of role or job that you would need to be doing in order to generate the annual income that you identified in the 'Finances' column. Try to identify the type of role rather than the specific job.	Record here your key strengths. Identify the minimum skills that are required in competently fulfilling the position that you identified in the 'Role' column.	Compare this with your own capabilities, as identified in the 'Skills' column and list the gaps between required and current.	Identify the personal development action that you need to take in order to develop and evidence the skills that you identified in the 'Gaps' column. Be specific. What will you do, when, with whom and how will you measure success.		Who is currently fulfilling the role to which you aspire? Are you able to use them as a role model? Are they someone who can demonstrate the skills required to fulfil their role successfully? What can you learn from them? How can they help you develop your skills gap?	Which individuals can you identify to assist you in achieving your development plan and attaining the roles that you aspire to?	Who can act as a sponsor for your ideas, your achievements and your ambitions?

Section 2
The Promise

What do you need to do?

This section of the book provokes you to make a promise to yourself of the action that you will take as a result of understanding yourself and your aims in life more fully. It is the 'So What?' test. It asks you some questions about how you are shaping your career and what you are renowned for. It stimulates you to define your Personal Brand Essence and become more aware of how your behaviours and actions are perceived by others.

8

Surviving and thriving in a corporate

"The beaten track does not lead to new pastures."
Indira Gandhi

An experiment was conducted at Washington DC Zoo with six chimpanzees. The keepers had built a new enclosure for the chimps and installed a stepladder in the centre of the enclosure, above which they had hung a juicy, ripe bunch of bananas. They let the monkeys into their new home and almost immediately one of them spotted the bananas. As he grabbed hold of the stepladder all six chimpanzees were hosed with ice cold water. Now, my knowledge of the animal kingdom is pretty much limited to the fabulous documentaries that we see on the television, but what I do know is that chimpanzees hate water. They will go to extreme lengths to avoid getting wet and this sudden drenching dissuaded them for several hours from going anywhere near the stepladder. Gradually though, they dried out and another of their number plucked up the courage to make a move for the stepladder. As he took hold of the first rung the keepers doused all six once again. This happened four times on the first day until the chimps gave up on the bananas. It was clearly a bad move.

On the second day, one of the original chimpanzees was removed and replaced with a new chimpanzee. The new chimpanzee immediately made a move for the stepladder, only to be hauled back by the remaining original five. No chimpanzees were hosed with water on any day other than the first. I cannot begin to imagine the conversation that ensued but the new monkey didn't go for the stepladder again. On the third day another original monkey was removed and a new chimp installed in its place. The new chimp made for the stepladder and all of the other five pulled him away from the stepladder, including the new chimpanzee from the previous day, even though he had never experienced the drenching that the others had.

And so this continued throughout the week. By the seventh day there were six chimpanzees in the enclosure, none of who had ever been hosed with water, none of whom ever went near the stepladder.

What, you may well ask, is going on here? Communication? Imitation? Conditioning? Evidently the experiment demonstrated that some form of communication was being used by the monkeys. It also demonstrated the willingness of the newcomers to be led by those already established in the group. They happily imitated their peers and quickly became conditioned to their way of behaving.

What fascinated me about the story was how analogous it was with human behaviour, particularly if we were to draw a parallel with when we first started working and more so if that were with a large corporate company. How often did you suggest an alternative way of doing something in the first few weeks and months of your working life? How often do you now hear a new starter in your organisation making similar challenges? Many of the challenges and suggestions made are borne out of inexperience, but equally validly, they are borne out of an objectivity that comes from not being conditioned by the way that the business has always done things.

The same often happens when we move into a new role. Because we don't know how everything works we make assumptions and suggestions based upon how we think it should work. Often these suggestions and ideas are hugely powerful and can save money, time and resources but they are often overlooked. Why? Because the response that is so frequently heard is; "Well, we don't do it like that around here."

The conversation in the monkey enclosure must have been similar. Imagine being the chimpanzee who was introduced on the seventh day, delighted at seeing fresh bananas hanging from the ceiling and a helpful ladder, handily placed below them. Then imagine your devastation at being told that you weren't allowed to grab a banana. On enquiring as to why this was the case of your five colleagues, none of who has ever had a soaking in the lives, you are told; "I don't know. We just don't do that around here."

What happens at work, of course, is that we withdraw into our shells with our foolish notions and ideas and gradually begin to allow ourselves to be conditioned by the behaviours of others around us and ultimately end up imitating them when the new kid on the block challenges us.

Now I would like to sound a note of caution here. We have already noted how dangerous motivated idiots can be. I am not suggesting that you throw caution and the rulebook to the wind, ignoring years and years of learning and experience. What I am suggesting is that it is too easy to allow your ideas to fall on fallow ground, or worse still, keep them yourself. I am not condoning taking risks that could ultimately bring your business tumbling down, I am condoning occasionally taking well thought through and considered risks in order to create impact and impetus. Don't just conform. Think and challenge, explore alternative ways forward and try new things out.

Joining a large corporation can be a daunting prospect to someone new to the workplace or to someone moving into a new role or making a career change. The fact that people don't know you and are not aware of your capabilities can engender an identity crisis to begin with. The sheer scale of some organisations can blinker employees and prevent them from fully exploiting their capabilities and the opportunities that the company offers.

This is where the work that we have done so far begins to play a part. By being aware of your strengths and weaknesses and developing your own personal brand you can start to make inroads into the corporate maze. Understanding how the business works and what makes the company successful enables you to identify where and how you can make a difference. Creating a Personal Development Plan that is designed to develop your commercial bandwidth and harness the power of your personal network helps enable you to fast track your way through the organisation.

You need to gain an understanding of the corporate politics within your company. Identify who the movers and shakers are and listen to them, watch them in action and learn from them. Develop ideas and opinions that are consistent with the aims of the business but that demonstrate and reinforce your individuality and the benefit that you personally bring to it.

Be in control of your own destiny and maximise the opportunities that you have to make an impression. Create impact through you ideas, your communication style and your behaviours. Consistently live up to you Personal Brand Essence.

I worked in a corporate organisation for over twenty years and I continue to work with corporate businesses almost every day through my work with *inspire*. Over the years I have developed a set of guidelines that I think are as equally important for people just starting work as they are for those already well entrenched.

Understand the key principles of business

Every organisation has a value chain. Companies buy things, they turn them into something and then they sell them. All businesses have a 'Buy Side' an 'In side' and a 'Sell side'. Take a retailer for example. They will source products and raw materials from suppliers. They will add some value to the products in the form of packaging and pricing or turn the raw materials into new merchandise. They will then sell these through their stores, or their catalogues or online. A bank will borrow money and then invest it in people, buildings and products. They will then offer mortgages, loans and insurance policies tailored to the needs of both their business customers and private individuals. A charity will recruit volunteers, raise money and then invest it into their cause.

To be able to add real value to the company that you work for you need to understand what the value chain in your organisation looks like. What are the procurement processes of your company? What does it buy? Who from? Why? How does your company improve upon the acquisitions that it makes? How does the business use them to improve its own effectiveness? What does it turn them into to sell? What does the business sell? Who to? Through which sales channels?

Understand what your company stands for and how that manifests itself in its brand. Understand how it markets itself, who its customers are and how it tries to differentiate itself from the competition. Understand what it is that your company sells and why its customers buy what it sells. Understand how your company is financed and how it manages its accounts. Be clear as to the difference between profit and cash. Know your share price and the yield that your company generates for its shareholders.

Once you know how the business works you will have a far greater appreciation of the role that you play within it. You will understand the importance of your cog within the overall machine. You will also be able to ask how things can be improved. You will be able to consider alternatives in the context of the overall business performance rather than from the isolation of your function. You will be able to make and implement your ideas and recommendations from a more objective perspective.

Prioritise your activity

You will remember your first day in your first job. You didn't know what to do and you had all day in which not to do it. You had plenty of time but didn't know how to fill it. Within weeks, if not days, your diary became full and you suddenly felt as though there wasn't enough time to get everything done. Once you have fallen into this trap it is very hard to escape from it. Much of our time is spent in a sand storm at work. We are blinded by the amount of work hitting our metaphorical in-tray. We are deafened by the noise of email and phone calls and the demands of customers, colleagues and managers. We feel as though we are being buried alive and then some soothsayer comes along and says "work smarter, not harder." Great. Thanks very much.

So how do we get out of this bear trap? Be clear about what are the vitally important parts of your job. Sit down and list everything that you do, then, prioritise the list. If it helps, go back to your job description and remind yourself of what you are there to do. You see the problem is not that we don't have enough time. The problem is that we do not do things in a prioritised way. We end up just snatching the next thing from the in-tray rather than planning and allocating enough time to do the important things. Everything is treated in the same way, whether it be a grain of sand, a pebble or a boulder. As a result we always seem to be in a state of flux, trying to keep all of the balls in the air at the same time. We often end up having to come back to some of our work and do it again because we didn't make the time to do it really well the first time around.

Cluster your list under three headings. The boulders are the really big things, the core components of your job. The pebbles are important tasks but would be pretty pointless if the boulders were not in place. The sand is everything else that needs to be done but ultimately is of secondary importance. There may even be some sand that you can shift. Go back through the last month of your diary and make a note of everything that you did. Now ask yourself, with the benefit of hindsight whether the time that you invested on each item was time well spent. You will find that this will help you with identifying your boulders and your pebbles but it will also weed out the things that you are currently doing that add no value. Stop doing them.

Go back to your diary and look at next month. You know what your boulders are and how long it takes you to do them. You know when they need to be done by and the order in which they need to be done. Put your boulders in your diary making enough time to do them well. Then drop in your pebbles following the same principles and finally, fill in the gaps with the remaining sand. Leave some space for the unexpected, for thinking time and for yourself.

Manage your time effectively

Are you a morning person or an afternoon person? When do you find that you are at your most productive? Many of us find that we are sharper in the morning; we find that words come easier to us when writing proposals or reports. We find that we can do things in less time than it would take in the afternoon because we feel sharper and more alert. For others the opposite applies in the afternoon. You will know best. So, where you have the opportunity to do so, plan your boulders into the part of the day when you know you are at your best. Not only will the quality of your work be better, you will probably find that you complete the task in less time.

Develop a 'one touch' rule. How often do you check your email in the course of a day? How often do you read an email and then mark it as unread or move it to another folder in order to deal with it again later in the day? How often do you allow an incoming phone call to interrupt your train of thought or make a phone call to someone else and have to leave a message because they are unavailable? If the nature of your work allows you to do so, allocate time in your daily schedule for email and phone calls. Check your email in the morning, at lunchtime and toward the end of the day. Wherever possible, deal with them as you read them. Turn down the volume of that noise. Switch off your email message pop up so that you can concentrate on the piece of work that you are doing and not be distracted by things that can wait their turn. Stop checking to see if you have had any emails every 30 minutes. If you were to add up the time that you spend just looking to see if you have received email you may find that you could have used that time to complete another task. Prioritise your email by colour coding email addresses and highlighting those from customers and managers. Put your phone on silent and then check your messages when you have planned to do so and call people back when you are likely to get them, at the beginning or at the end of the day. If it is urgent they will usually text you.

Attend fewer meetings. Now that may sound like a step too far, but just consider for a moment how much time you spend in meetings. Now consider for how much of that time you were proactively involved in those meetings. Set yourself some rules for meetings and try to abide by them whether you are attending or hosting. The meeting should have clear objectives that are supported with a time bound agenda. Action points arising from the meeting should be circulated and acted upon within the agreed timescales. Attendees should be given time to prepare for the meeting and have a specific reason for attending. Ask for an agenda. Only attend for the part of the meeting that is relevant to you. Do not attend or host a meeting where there is not a clearly defined output. Act upon the commitments that you make at the meeting. Consider if the meeting can be conducted virtually instead of face to face. Would an audio or videoconference get the same result as well as saving the time and cost involved in getting everyone into the same room? Remember to apply the same rules to these virtual meetings as you would to face to face meetings.

Try to let go of work at the end of every day. We all need to be able to switch off and not take the strains and stresses home with us. I find that writing a 'to do list' at the end of every day helps me with this. It provides closure and gives me the peace of mind that I will not forget to do what needs to be done tomorrow. Remember how important it is to prioritise the list and to focus on the boulders first. Some people have a habit of leaving the big thing until last and then find that they do not have time to complete it fully. Don't just write a list. I use post-its so that I can move things around if unexpected things hit the in tray.

Build a reputation of reliability, of doing what you say you will do. By making time to do things well, first time, every time, you will be able to set expectations and deliver against them.

Develop your communication skills

Most of our peers have the same experience as us. They come from similar backgrounds to us, have benefited from the same education as us and have comparable qualifications to us. I believe that one of the few ways in which people can truly differentiate from their contemporaries is through the skill of communication, of imparting one's own views and ideas. There is no doubt in my mind that people who can communicate well, get on and move up within organisations.

In my early days at BT the thought of standing up and speaking in front of a group of people filled me with dread. I was so preoccupied by what people would think of me that I actively avoided the opportunities to do so when they materialised. What struck me after a while was that the people who did take advantage of the opportunity were nearly always the same people who progressed within the business. It dawned on me that this was not just because they were confident enough in their own abilities to stand up and speak, they were able to give people the benefit of their beliefs and opinions when they did so. The audience would listen to their suggestions and recommendations and many would be influenced by them. Their brand was on display and people formed perceptions of them as a result. They were advertising themselves and the outcome of those adverts was that they stood out more than me and their talents and capabilities were more readily recognised.

If you have any ambitions to progress in a company you have to be able to structure and deliver your message with impact. You must confront your demons and master the art of presenting. If not, you will not get the platform that you need and deserve. You will not be heard.

Build a personal network

Personal networks provide us with three things. They help us to increase our own personal awareness through feedback, criticism and coaching. They improve our wealth of knowledge and commercial bandwidth as a result of exposure to different skill sets, opinions and experience. They provide us with potential opportunity as the people within our personal networks will hopefully, have formed positive opinions of us over the years and may well be in positions of influence.

We all already have a personal network. It is populated by friends and family, associates and acquaintances. People who offer us advice and guidance, based upon expertise and experience that we do not yet have ourselves. When we join a company it is essential that we get to know people. If you follow the suggestions that I made earlier in this chapter when we looked at understanding the key principles of business, you will have spoken to a lot of people. These people will potentially also become members of your personal network. Keep in touch with them and develop and nurture those relationships.

Networking plays a crucial part in personal success at work. People enable things to happen. Contacts smooth the way and make it easier for you to get things done. As they progress, they themselves become more influential within the business. The relationships that you forged with them in the past will potentially open doors for you in the future. We will look at how you build your personal network in more detail in Chapter 13.

Demonstrate the right behaviours

Build your brand. Be professional and work hard. Have fun and allow your personality to flourish but remember that there is a time and a place for everything. Demonstrate flexibility and a hunger to succeed. Volunteer for things and offer to get involved in project work and with virtual teams. Demonstrate a willingness to learn by seeking feedback and guidance as well as spending time understanding the business and talking to people from other disciplines.

Believe in yourself and your capabilities. Trust in your own instinct and have the courage of your convictions as long as you know that they have been well thought through. Don't give up at the first sign of rejection; be persistent. Don't let others take credit for your ideas. Make sure that people know that the idea came from you. Demonstrate stamina by pacing yourself. It is important that people see a consistency of performance rather than peaks and troughs. Be enthusiastic and positive. Wear a smile on your face and look for solutions not just problems. Choose to do something about it rather than be another victim.

Oh, and go and grab a banana once in a while!

So What?

- Having worked in or with corporates and large organisation for the best part of thirty years now I have developed a personal set of guidelines that I believe help people survive and thrive in the business arena, whether they are just starting out or whether they are well established.

1. Understand the key principles of business
2. Prioritise your activity
3. Manage your time effectively
4. Develop your communication skills
5. Build a personal network
6. Demonstrate the right behaviours

9

What will you be famous for?

"It had long since come to my attention that people of accomplishment rarely sat back and let things happen to them. They went out and happened to things."
Leonardo da Vinci

I was working with a friend and mentor of mine, Greg Philips, scripting and rehearsing my presentation for my first end of year sales conference as a General Manager. We were working on the structure of my messages and he asked me what I wanted the legacy of the conference to be. What was the one thing, amongst all of the messages that the audience would hear, that I wanted them to leave with, ringing in their ears. Looking back, it was another defining moment in my own personal development.

I wasn't certain of the answer and pushed back by arguing that I only got this audience together once a year and there was so much that I needed to tell them that it wasn't possible to just have a single message. That, he told me, was the problem with most conferences. There are too many messages; no clearly defined purpose. As a result the audience departs with a mishmash of thoughts and a feeling of same, same but different.

We worked on the problem and tried to come up with a single resounding provocation that they would leave with and act upon as a result.

Our conversation stimulated deeper thoughts within me. If I was finding it hard to define the legacy of a sales conference, how much more difficult would it be to define my own legacy. I was 36 years old and felt suddenly as though I hadn't really achieved anything of real note in my life. Greg's wise counsel continued and he asked me what the difference was that I made to the people around me. Not just with the people that I worked with, but with my friends and my family. I didn't know. I had a feeling of what it was, but I was not able to articulate it. I couldn't put it into words and point at examples to reinforce it. I hadn't really thought about it at all before. I asked Greg what he felt his legacy was. "My children," he said, "they will be my legacy."

It didn't matter if his answer to my conundrum worked for me or not. The important thing was that it worked for him. You could tell by the glint in his eye and the way that he said it that he was absolutely certain and very content with what his legacy was. I could not have Greg's legacy anyway, because it was unique to him. It was based on all of the things that he had consciously done to create it, all of the things that were special, exclusive and intimate to him.

To be fair, there was also a significant reason as to why I couldn't adopt Greg's legacy as my own. At that time I didn't have any children of my own and I was not satisfied to defer until I did. There were other reasons too. I wanted to leave my own legacy, I wanted to contribute something and I wanted to make a difference.

I began by trying to define what the difference was that made a difference to the people with whom I interacted. I started with my colleagues, my team and my customers at work. I then considered my close friends and family and the other people with whom I socialised. I asked myself what they would say if they were defining the one resounding thing that I was best known for. Then, I asked them. I cannot say that I liked the answers. They were polite and considerate enough but they were hugely inconsistent. These inconsistencies did not just manifest themselves between work and pleasure; they were significantly different from one customer to another, from one colleague to another and from one friend to another. It was clear to me that if I was to become famous for something I had to consciously go out and create it and consistently reinforce it through my actions and behaviours.

So I set about creating it. I identified what I was good at. I formed clearer opinions on the things that I thought were important both at home and at work. I acted upon those opinions and tried to make changes to the way that I lived and worked. I put into place a series of changes in the way that my part of the business was run. I began to implement many of the ideas that I had formed over the years of my apprenticeship and followed my instincts. I needed to create some personal vehicles for myself. Things that people would associate with Steve Connell. Things that others would begin to emulate and build upon. I monitored and measured the impact of the changes that I had made by collecting evidence of improvements (and downturns) in sales performance, customer satisfaction and employee satisfaction.

I had decided that I wanted my legacy to be that I had made a difference. That everybody with whom I came into contact would feel differently as a result. I wanted to be a catalyst for change. I wanted to provoke people into improving their lives. I wanted people to feel inspired, motivated and compelled to take action. The change in me as a person was noticeable. It gave me confidence, self-belief and focus. It gave me the courage and commitment to make changes in my personal life as well as at work. It ultimately led to me setting up *inspire*, a business focused upon doing just that.

So, as part of your promise, ask yourself these questions.

- What are you known for saying and doing?
- How would people describe your legacy right now?
- What contribution do you make at work?
- What are the big ideas that you could implement at work?
- What difference do you make to your friends and family?
- What is the difference that makes you the difference?
- What evidence do you have to support that?
- How will you make your mark?
- What do you want your legacy to be?
- What would you want your epitaph to read?

Now, make it happen. Do something about it. Take control of your life and become the master of your own destiny.

So What?

- If you don't know what you want your legacy to be what chance is there of leaving one?

- What is the difference that makes you the difference?

- What are the promises that you make to yourself every day?

- What is your current reputation?

- What would you like it to be?

- What will you be remembered for?

- Take control of your life and become the master of your own destiny.

10

Defining your Personal Brand Essence

*"The great danger for most of us is not that our aim is
too high and we miss, but that it is too low and we
achieve it."*
Michelangelo

If you don't know what you stand for, how can you behave in a way
that exemplifies it? If I were to ask your best friend for the one word
that defines you, what would they say? If I were to ask your partner
the same question, or your boss, would they give me the same word?
If not, why not? Would the word that they gave me be the one that
you would want them to say? If not, why not?

We need to be certain of what our Personal Brand Essence is
before we can begin to project it, before we can advertise it through
our actions and behaviours.

The actual process of defining your Personal Brand Essence is
pretty straightforward. The task itself is a little more complex and
time consuming. However, the outcome is massively worthwhile, as
it provides you with a touchstone that you can refer to whenever you
need to in order to remind yourself of who you are and how your
need to react to certain situations in order to reinforce the perceptions
that you are trying to create.

Ideally, you need to come up with a single word, preferably an adjective rather than a noun, that summarises you and the essence of your personal brand. The more unusual and descriptive the word is the better. You can, of course, have more than one word but I find that it really helps to concentrate on distilling it down to a single point of reference. Ultimately it is what the word means to you personally that is of real importance rather than the actual word itself, but you cannot provide the meaning without first identifying the source of that meaning.

Before trying to establish which word best represents your Personal Brand Essence remind yourself of the business brand that you selected when we were exploring what brand is in Chapter 1. I have found that by doing this it helps people to understand what I am driving at. It encourages them to get under the skin of a brand and really think about what the brand is trying to say to you.

You may have ended up with a combination of brands. This is because we take the things that we like from certain brands and ignore the things that we don't like. Ultimately, of course, you are your own brand. By definition you cannot be a subset of another brand or a combination of brands. You are unique and just as everyone has their own distinctive DNA so does everyone have their own distinctive, unique and differentiating Personal Brand Essence.

Authenticity is vital. We have to be true to ourselves and ensure that the brand that we are trying to create and bring to life through our behaviours is genuine, relevant and authentic. If it is fake then people will see through it. It would be very difficult to create a set of behaviours that one could consistently implement against a brand that was ultimately untrue. If it is real then the behaviours will come naturally and our natural behaviours will only be enhanced through the new one's that we consciously adopt.

To get you started on trying to come up with the single word that defines your Personal Brand Essence it may also be helpful to refer back to the notes that you made in Chapter 3. Here you will have recorded your attributes, your physical characteristics. You will have noted the benefits that people feel as a result of interacting with you. You will know which values are most important to you. You will have a greater appreciation of your own personal experience, of your skills and capabilities as well as the way that you behave and the things that you do and say. The words that you have used to describe your personality will have defined what makes you, you.

You will also find it very useful to have a dictionary and a thesaurus close at hand.

Take your list of words and one by one and look up the definition of them in a good dictionary. You will find that there are other words that leap off of the page, out of the definition, that resonate with you even more. Add those words to your list, refining it as you go. It is important that you choose words that you like the sound of, words that attract you and define themselves in the same way that you interpret the word. After all, you have to like your own brand!

People sometimes fall between two stools at this stage. They are not certain whether they should choose a brand essence which sums them up as they perceive themselves to be now, or whether they should be searching for a word that defines the way that they want to be in the future. My advice is to be aspirational, but to be realistic as well. You cannot decide that from tomorrow you will mostly be 'Churchillian'. Not only would the initial shock be too great for some people, they will eventually see through it in the future, particularly in times of stress or pressure, as you will not be able to live up to something that is not fundamentally representative of you. Ultimately, you are you, and the Personal Brand Essence that you choose has to be reflective of who you are. You cannot fundamentally change your personality and you should not choose a word that is entirely alien to you, your personality and your character. However, you can choose a word that stretches you, that reminds you of the promise that you are making to yourself and that reinforces what you need to do to in order to live up to the perception and emotion that you are trying to create. Just remember that you have to live up to it through your actions and your behaviours.

Once you have distilled your list then use your thesaurus to seek out more dynamic, descriptive and unusual words to use as better alternatives. What you will begin to notice is that the same few words keep appearing as recommended alternatives. You are starting to get to the answer.

When I was a child, Christmas was a very special time in our home. My Mum would treat the five kids to a tin of Quality Street, which would be rationed in order to last throughout the seasonal festivities. Each evening we could all choose one chocolate from the tin and I always employed the same selection process. I would take one of each sort of the remaining chocolates and line them up side by side. I would then remove the one that I liked the least and continue until I had to make a choice from the final two. The fact that this was always a choice between the Green Triangle and the Purple Hazelnut Caramel was irrelevant. I found the process necessary to convince myself that I had made the 'best' choice and it helped to console me when those favourites of mine were no longer available. In the same way, force yourself to remove words from your list as you sharpen the pencil. Choose between one word or another basing your choice on which word is more descriptively accurate of you.

Don't be tempted to use generic words. Remember that you are trying to find something that is authentic and true to you, but that also distinguishes you from the masses and that best summarises the way in which you differentiate yourself from others. Words such as professional, caring and charismatic are not explicit enough. They will apply to too many other people and you may be tempted to interpret them in a way that you see others rather than the way that you see yourself.

What you are attempting to do is not easy and in order to try and help I want to share my Personal Brand Essence with you, as well as the process that I went through to arrive at it.

You will recall that what I wanted to be famous for was making a difference to people. I wanted to be a catalyst for change by provoking people and compelling them to take action.

I started by making a list of the key words that appealed and applied to me. I started with:

- Catalyst
- Change
- Provoke
- Compel

111

I went back to the words that I had selected as my own Personal Brand Essence components and added the following:

Attributes:
Big. Confident. Positive.

Benefits:
Motivated. Enthused. Inspired.

Values:
Integrity. Fairness. Honesty.

Experience:
Credible. Knowledgeable. Proven.

Behaviours:
Reliable. Consistent. Different.

Personality:
Gregarious. Extrovert. Happy.

I had a list of twenty-two words to work with. I looked up the definition of all of the words in the dictionary and with the help of a thesaurus, started to select alternative, more attractive and unusual words with which to work.

- A catalyst '**provokes** a reaction'.
- Change is 'an act of making a difference'.
- To provoke is to 'incite and **arouse**'.
- Compel gave me '**rousing** strong interest'.
- Big is defined as 'of considerable size and **intensity**'.
- Confidence is about being 'self assured and bold'.
- Positive gave me '**definitive** and unquestionable'.
- Motivate '**inspire** a person to act'.
- Enthusiasm is about 'great eagerness'.

- Inspire is defined as '**arousing** creative activity'.
- Integrity offered me 'wholeness and soundness'.
- Fairness is defined as 'just, unbiased and equitable'.
- Honesty is ' fair and just in character and behaviour'.
- Credible offers 'believable and convincing'.
- Knowledgeable is defined as 'well informed, intelligent'.
- Proven is about 'demonstrating through evidence'.
- Reliable is being 'of sound and consistent character'.
- Consistency is being 'harmonious and non-contradictory'.
- Different is defined as being '**distinct** and separate'.
- Gregarious people are 'fond of company'.
- Extroverts are 'outgoing and sociable people'.
- Happy people 'show pleasure and contentment'.

I now had a new list of words, generated through my research, from my original list. I deliberately refined and reduce the words on the new list to those that really appealed to me in a more descriptive and proactive way.

My new list was:

- Provoke
- Arouse
- Intensity
- Definitive
- Motivate
- Inspire
- Distinct

I was drawn to the word 'inspire' but I wanted to prove it right by exploring my new list of words a little further. I used the thesaurus again looking for evidence.

'Provoke' offered the following alternatives; incite, rouse, cause, bring about, trigger and stir.

'Arouse' gave me **inspire**. 'Stir' gave me **inspire**.

'Intensity' offered 'passion' as an alternative which offered 'enthusiasm' and this, in turn, offered **inspire**.

113

'Definitive' offered ultimate, perfect and best. Attractive words admittedly, but perhaps a little arrogant and unrealistic to have as a Personal Brand Essence.

'Motivate' gave me enthuse, stimulate, stir, encourage, provoke and **inspire**. Enthuse gave me **inspire**. Stimulate gave me arouse, stir and **inspire**. Arouse gave me **inspire**. Stir gave me **inspire**. Encourage gave me **inspire**.

'Distinct' gave me unique, distinctive and individual, just like my Personal Brand Essence needed to be.

'Inspire' was the word that I chose.

I loved the word. As a final check and balance I grabbed the dictionary and looked up its definition: *To stimulate and arouse creative activity. To instil and create feelings in people.* I was hooked. It represented beautifully what I was trying to achieve. It was how I would go about trying to make a difference to people, by inspiring them to make changes both in their attitude and their skills to realise their personal goals and professional ambitions. In fact, I liked it so much it was what I chose to call my company.

What, of course, is of most importance is how I use the word in the course of my everyday life.

'Inspire' is the last word that I think to myself every time that I walk on to a stage, or enter a classroom or into a meeting with a client.

'Inspire' is the word that enters my head when I am confronted by a difficult, awkward or pressurised situation. It helps me to choose the way that I will react to that situation.

In the course of my work I will often use the word rhetorically. How do I make a proposal inspirational? How do I make a presentation inspirational? How do I dress inspirationally? What vocabulary do I use to inspire people?

It impacts upon the way that I interact with people professionally and socially. It reminds me to smile and to listen and to show interest in other people.

It works for me because it gives me a single touchstone to use whenever I need to call upon it. It shifts my personal brand into my consciousness and demands that I act and behave in a way that is consistent with it.

I know what I mean when I think it. I know what I mean when I say it.

Exactly the same applies to others with whom I have worked on developing their own Personal Brand Essence. They too have found that by identifying the word (or words) that is most representative of them, and of how they wish to be perceived, has enabled them to focus on developing a set of consistent behaviours.

Once you have identified your Personal Brand Essence you can then set about reviewing your current behaviours and ask yourself three questions. Firstly, which of my existing behaviours are consistent with the Personal Brand Essence that I am trying to project? These are the behaviours that you should keep. Secondly, which of my existing behaviours are inconsistent with the perceptions that I am trying to create? These are the behaviours that you should stop. Thirdly, what do I need to do to help reinforce and build upon my Personal Brand Essence? These are the behaviours that you need to start.

It may help to share with you some 'case studies' in order to further illustrate how particularly effective the 'right' word can be in identifying which behaviours to keep, stop and start.

Case Study 1. Susannah
Personal Brand Essence: 'Sunshine'

Susannah always has a smile on her face. She is positive, optimistic and cheerful she is well known for her upbeat attitude and style. Although not a senior manager, she is often relied upon by her company to implement fairly complex projects in a number of diverse areas. She has a track record for delivery and her managers know that she will commit herself fully to any task with the aim of doing it well and to the best of her abilities.

Susannah settled upon 'sunshine' as her Personal Brand Essence. She described what it meant to her as; always bright and warming, lighting the path and leading the way, nurturing, refreshing and helping things to grow. She knew what she meant. She knew what she needed to do to turn that perception into reality.

Susannah is proud of her reputation. She knows that people rely on her to do a good job and will give her the autonomy that she enjoys to do it her way. She wants to keep performing well and building upon this reputation.

She decided that she wanted to stop saying 'yes' to things too readily. Because of her willingness to be involved she often found herself to be over burdened with things to do. Susannah is aware that by taking on too much in order to please others, she may end up failing to deliver against their expectations and therefore damage her brand and reputation as a result.

She determined that she needed to start working on her gravitas. Yes, she is well liked and popular but occasionally, people seem not to take her or her ideas as seriously as she would like. She occasionally feels as though she is taken for granted and that her efforts, experience and knowledge not always fully appreciated.

Susannah doesn't want to lose her 'sunshine' brand but wants to make sure that people recognise that she can shed light on problems and challenges and that she can be a guiding light as well as a willing implementer.

Case Study 2. Gareth
Personal Brand Essence: 'Fifth Avenue'

Gareth is a big, strapping rugby player. He loves being at the centre of things. His job is company-wide and as a result he comes into contact with many people in many different parts of the business. He is motivated by recognition and achievement. He is ambitious and wants to accomplish great things both personally and professionally.

He was, of course, thinking of Fifth Avenue in Manhattan, New York City when he made his choice. He described Fifth Avenue as being at the epicentre of one of the most powerful, alluring and well known cities in the world. He described that what it meant to him was; big and strong, established and at the heart of things; where people want to walk; where giants live.

He knew what he meant. He wanted to be at the heart of things. He wanted to establish himself professionally. He wanted to be seen as an achiever who scaled great heights. He wanted to rub shoulders with other great achievers.

Gareth decided that he wanted to keep building his personal network. It was a natural talent of his and he already enjoyed good working relationships with many of his colleagues. He recognised that it is vital for him to create new contacts and build upon his existing relationships with key people within his business. This would help him to maintain and enhance his reputation and potentially open up new professional opportunities in the future.

He wanted to stop jumping from one project to another without ever quite finishing anything and demonstrating the full value that had come from his work. He appreciated that tall buildings need strong foundations and that one of the things that he needed to stop doing was failing to finish building the foundations before moving on to newer, more exciting tasks.

He wanted to start identifying the specific actions that he needed to take in order to establish himself at the top of his company. He recognised that he needed to have a master plan and the he needed to take specific action in order to move on within his organisation. He needed to start taking some considered, deliberate and conscious moves in order to propel his career forward more effectively.

Case Study 3. Charlotte
Personal Brand Essence – 'Freedom'

Charlotte is a senior manager in a well-known multinational company. She has gradually worked her way up the corporate ladder by moving from one company to another, having established herself in each new company and built upon her reputation by consistently delivering against her objectives and exceeding the expectations of her bosses.

She has been considering, for some time now, creating a better work life balance for herself. She has always prided herself on being financially independent and not being tied to a particular company or role. She likes being able to do want she wants to, when it suits her and whilst she recognises the need for a degree of sobriety, when the occasion demands, she doesn't like to be pigeon-holed or stereotyped in anyway. She sees herself as a free spirit.

Charlotte chose the word 'freedom' because she felt that it was highly representative of the way that she had lived her life so far and of the way that she wanted to live it in the future.

When it came to her behaviours, she wanted to keep seeking out new working challenges and looking for opportunities in different types of businesses to stretch and improve herself. However, there was a need for the new roles to be more flexible from a time perspective, to allow her the freedom to explore new avenues such as voluntary work, travelling and charitable activity.

She wanted to stop putting off the time when she focussed more on what she could achieve outside of the work place. She recognised that as time slipped by so the opportunity of encountering new life experiences diminished and whilst there is always a need to balance earning a living with living life the time had come to take some proactive decisions to enable this to happen.

She wanted to start giving something back. She wanted to start working on projects that concentrated on improving the lots of others less fortunate than herself. This personal aspiration could also be coupled with her long held love of overseas travel. She wanted the freedom to do these things now and not at some undefined time in the future.

Charlotte's Personal Brand Essence of 'freedom' had always been in her consciousness. However, having taken the time to deliberately define it as well as ask herself how she was going to bring it to life more overtly, it became the catalyst for her to make some decisions and choices rather than promises to herself to do something at some stage in the future.

Case Study 4. Peter
Personal Brand Essence: 'Panache'

Peter is a flamboyant and stylish character with real flare. He is like a butterfly in many ways. He dresses to kill and is always wearing the latest fashions. He flits from one job to another, one city to another and one apartment to another. He is supremely confident and has the 'gift of the gab' and can talk his way in to and out of most things. He is constantly searching for new opportunities, new experiences and new challenges. He loved the challenge of coming up with a Personal Brand Essence for himself and concentrated very much around highly visual words as he searched through dictionaries and thesauruses.

Ultimately he came up with the word 'Panache'. He loved the very sound of the word, the continental overtones, not to mention the dictionary definition of *flamboyant confidence of style or manner.*

Identifying which behaviours to keep, stop and start proved a little more challenging for Peter. He is still young and enjoying finding his way and as such, was not overly keen to restrict himself too much. Nevertheless he did recognise the importance of refining his image and his focus somewhat and decided upon the following.

He was going to keep living life to the full, looking for new working opportunities and personal experiences. He planned to stop taking so many 'off the cuff' decisions based upon impulse rather than taking all of the pro's and con's into consideration. He decided to start focusing his seemingly limitless energies into defining a career path and elected to begin by creating his own Personal Life Plan.

Many people with whom I have worked have not only enjoyed taking some time out to think about themselves in the context of a brand. To a man and woman, they have also found that by specifying what it is that they believe to be their personal brand word has enabled them to make some decisions about their behaviours with greater clarity, purpose and conviction.

The great news is that, whatever the word is that you have chosen, it is the right word. By definition, the Personal Brand Essence that you have selected for yourself has to be correct. After all, you have chosen it as the single word that is most representative of your personality and that most accurately defines you. You know what you mean when you use the word to describe yourself. It is distinctive and differentiating and the meaning of it is unique to you.

I have found that the power of being able to define it is that it becomes a constant reminder to oneself of the way to behave. It is not a word that you have tattooed on your forehead for all to see. It is a word that reinforces in your own mind the way in which you should react to situations that arise, the way that you should deal with people, the way you should act, the way that you should dress, the way that you should speak, the language and vocabulary that you should use.

People occasionally ask me if they can change their Personal Brand Essence once they have selected it. As we mature, we become wiser and more experienced. We may choose to change direction in our personal or business lives when we reach crossroads in our journey. As a result our Personal Brand Essence will evolve and we may feel that we need to change the word that we have selected in order to use something that is more descriptive of where we now find ourselves and of the new challenges that we face. Of course we can change it, so long as the evolution remains representative of us, of our essence. The point is not so much the word that we choose but what that word means to us.

People often ask me if they need a different Personal Brand Essence for work compared with the one that they use at home or with friends. My answer is always the same. Your Personal Brand Essence is your Personal Brand Essence wherever you are and whomever you are with. It has to be. You cannot fundamentally be three different people. What is different, of course, is the way that you behave and the ways that your Personal Brand Essence manifests itself. I try to be inspirational at work, at home and when I am with my friends. I just try to do it in different ways.

People always ask me once they have defined their Personal Brand Essence, what they should do with it. This is what we will explore in the final section of the book. Bringing your brand to life in 'The Performance'.

So What?

- If you are able to distil your Personal Brand Essence into a single word it will help you to adopt behaviours that are reflective of your brand and the perception that you are trying to create.

- Identify three behaviours that you will adopt or adapt as a result of defining your Personal Brand Essence.

- What one thing will you keep doing that is entirely consistent with your brand?

- What one thing will you stop doing which conflicts with the perceptions that you are trying to create in others?

- What one thing will you start doing to proactively bring your Personal Brand Essence to life more overtly?

Section 3
The Performance

How will you do it?

This section of the book asks how you intend to go about implementing your plan and delivering upon the promise that you have made to yourself. It looks at how you project your brand to your different audiences. It helps you to identify the behaviours that you need to modify and develop in order to reinforce the brand that you have defined. It prompts you to think about your style, your attitude and your appearance. It helps you to create personal impact and to build commercial bandwidth.

11

Living your brand

"You must be the change that you want to see in the world."
Mahatma Gandhi

I have been lucky enough to work with many gifted people. Skilful people that excelled brilliantly in their chosen fields. One such person was an outstanding sales manager, probably the best that I have ever worked with. He was a true sales professional. His appearance was immaculate. His product knowledge was second to none. The rigour with which he followed the sales processes was exemplary. His ability to build relationships with his customers and to create bespoke solutions to match their requirements consistently put him at the top of sales leagues. But in the evening his demeanour would change. When he was 'off duty' he was a different man. He became raucous and lewd after just a couple of pints and descended into a drunken, womanising mess as the evening progressed. He was a true Jekyll and Hyde character. How do you think people remember him?

Brand is reinforced through behaviour. The moment that a brand conveys something that fails to live up to our expectations of that brand is the moment that we begin to change the way that we feel about the brand.

Consider for a moment where you buy your food or, where you buy your clothes or, the car that you drive. The brand of the company

124

that you choose to use makes a promise to you. You expect it to live up to the standards that you have grown accustomed to. Imagine if the quality or quantity of the ingredients in the food that you bought began to diminish. Imagine if the clothes that you bought began to fray or weaken at the seams. Imagine if the car that you bought became unreliable and began to let you down, leaving you stranded on the hard shoulder of the motorway. Would you continue to use that brand or would you look to switch to an alternative brand?

The same applies to us as individuals. The perceptions that we are trying to create have to be mirrored in our behaviours. If we are trying to create a certain perception and fail to demonstrate the associated behaviours then we create a disparity between perception and reality. If we have successfully established a reputation and then begin to behave in a different way, the way that people regard us will change. Reputations can be damaged in the blink of an eye. What has taken years to create can be undermined by one moment of thoughtlessness or carelessness.

A man becomes his habits. Our habits become our behaviours. Many of our habits are subconscious, we perform them without thinking and as a result the way that we behave, particularly in times of stress, is predetermined, conditioned by the way that we have always reacted to certain situations. Ask yourself if you are happy with the perception that your reactions create in people. Ask yourself if you have ever reacted to a situation or said something in the heat of the moment that you have later regretted? I believe that we need to become more consciously aware of how we react and how we behave. We have to think about the consequences of our behaviours and ask ourselves whether they reinforce the brand perception that we are trying to create or clash with it, potentially damaging our brand as a result.

We need to ensure that our habits are good and that we improve our behaviours. We need to recondition ourselves by consistently asking ourselves what people will think of our reaction, how will it influence their perception of us and how consistent is it with our Personal Brand Essence.

So how do we go about reconditioning ourselves?

Identify the pillars that support your behaviours and review them one by one. Distinguish between the behaviours that are consistent with your Personal Brand Essence and that reinforce the way that you define it and the behaviours that fail to support it. Create a list of behaviours that you should stop doing, keep doing and start doing.

Revisit the components of your Personal Brand Essence and ask yourself which behaviours would be most representative of the words that you have selected to describe yourself.

Stop behaving in ways that damage your brand. Think about the things that you have done and later regretted. Stop doing them. Listen to the feedback that people give you. If they tell you that something you do annoys them then stop doing it. Keep doing the things that you know reinforce your brand. Start developing new behaviours that are consistent with the brand perception that you wish to create.

There is a book, written by W. Chan Kim and Reneé Mauborgne called *Blue Ocean Strategy*. It promotes the concept of creating new and uncontested market space referred to as 'blue ocean'. By using the metaphor of blue and red oceans the authors suggest that many of today's most successful businesses have created business strategies that set themselves distinctly apart from their competitors. In the red oceans, existing players have predetermined the competitive boundaries and the rules of the game are already known. However, in blue oceans, market space is undefined and unexplored and demand is created rather than fought over. This demand is created through 'value innovation' and the more innovative the business is – the more successful it becomes.

A former boss of mine, Simon Kelly, introduced me to the concept and explained how he had adopted the provocation made by the book into his own personal behaviours. When he joined BT there was a culture of being 'suited and booted'. Collar and tie were part of the corporate dress code. Simon made a conscious decision to start dressing in a different way. He dressed down. He was always smart but he decided to dress differently. He wore open neck shirts, tailored trousers and sports jackets. People noticed. Simon didn't just dress differently. He spoke differently, he presented differently, he challenged people differently. He wasn't a maverick, well, not in the true sense of the word, but he was close to it. He stood out from the crowd in his thoughts, in his deeds and in his attire.

After a while, Simon began to notice that others were beginning to adopt the same dress code that he had implemented as one of his personal blue ocean behaviours. His ocean was becoming redder as his competition began to invade the space that he had created. So, he changed his behaviour again and created new blue ocean with his sharp suits and silk ties.

Personally I like the concept. It provoked me to think about how innovative I could be in the new behaviours that I decided to adopt. It provoked me to think more about how I could be more proactive in setting myself apart from my competitors.

Which part of the ocean will you choose to swim in?

It is essential that we are **adaptable**. We need to create our own space and our own identity but we also need to be willing to refresh our brand and evolve as a result. Our competitive environment is constantly changing and in order to be distinctive we need to differentiate and adapt our behaviours to meet the requirements of different situations and connect with people.

I have outlined below, some of the behaviours that I have tried to adopt since defining my own Personal Brand Essence. Some of them may stir some thoughts in you and provoke you to include them in your list, but they are intended to give you an example against which you can create your own 'start list'.

Become more consultative

My definition of a consultant is a simple one. A consultant is someone who has an opinion. In order to have formed an opinion we will have had to gain an understanding of the subject, researched it and decided upon our point of view before being able to confidently articulate it and back it up with evidence if required to do so. Raise your head once in a while and try to absorb the bigger picture. Form opinions about it and impart them when relevant to do so. If you form opinions, people will begin to ask you for them. They will value your input and consult you more often.

Be positive

Look for ways that challenges can be overcome and not for reasons as to why they cannot. Many people seem to have a gift of being able to identify problems. I often hear the phrase; "they always get that wrong" (whoever 'they' are). It is easy to sit back and criticise, easy to say that you would have gone about things differently. So, don't just come up with problems, but think about how you would address those problems and offer your recommendations. Put yourselves in the shoes of others and try to provide them with an alternative perspective.

Make time for people

I once heard of a manager who would walk through the call centre in the morning without so much as a nod to any of his team on his way to his office at the far end of the floor. Once at his desk he would send an email to everyone on the floor wishing them a good morning. Imagine how that made his team feel. What would it have cost him to stop and chat to just a few different members of his team each morning when he arrived in the office?

I was in the habit of saving my best for the meeting that I was about to have with my client. I wasn't rude to other people, but I rarely made time to speak to the doorman, or the cleaner, or the receptionist. I failed to acknowledge other people who I encountered in the lift or passed in the corridor on the way to the meeting with even a smile. Fortunately, my chickens never came home to roost but there have been many occasions that the people I blanked ended up being the people with whom I worked through the detail of the meeting that I had just had with the head honcho. What an advantage I would have had if I had already established a rapport with those people and created a positive perception in their mind.

Be nice to people

Make people feel important. Smile at them, take a few moments to linger with them. Really concentrate on them when you are speaking with them. Face them and look into their eyes. Show a real interest in what they are saying. Listen to what they say and comment relevantly. It is so easy just to say good morning or good afternoon to people. It costs nothing but a few seconds of your day to ask, genuinely, how somebody is. It pays to remember to say please and thank you.

It is, of course, equally easy to forget to do all of these things. We are busy, often in a hurry and deep in our own thoughts. My point is that the things that you do not do, say just as much about you as the things that you do, do.

Keep in touch with people

Just think for a moment about all of the people that have at some time or another played a part in your life. The friends that you had at school, the people who were a part of your childhood circles. The colleagues that formed the team that you first worked within, the people who gave you your first career break and those that helped you take advantage of it.

I reckon that most people keep in touch with fewer than ten per cent of the people that they, at one time or another, would have described as their friends. I guess it is one of the attractions of school reunions and social networking sites. Where are you now? What have you done? What are you doing now?

Call people when you think about them. Call people for no other reason than to say hello. Too many people only contact former friends and colleagues when they need a favour. Drop them a line or even a text or an email on their birthday. Send them a Christmas card. It makes people feel special and it makes you feel good. And, if the time does come that you need a favour, it won't feel or appear as though that is the only time that you ever think about them.

Be consistent

We have all worked with people who are susceptible to being a little moody. Occasionally these mood swings are so dramatic that we are not quite sure how to handle them and we will often go to extreme lengths to avoid the person if at all possible. Don't be a 'mood hoover' yourself. Choose your attitude and choose how you will react to situations. Choose your mood every day. Make a conscious decision to play from a 10 out of 10 and do not let small, irrelevant irritations allow you to drop from your 10. Don't take your personal troubles to work with you and don't take your business pressures home with you.

Ask good questions

Be inquisitive and seek information. It supports the behaviour of being more consultative and at the same time increases your personal knowledge and commercial bandwidth. Find out how things work and spend time considering how you could improve upon them. Remember to use open-ended questions as they counteract assumptions, encourage thought and provide you with better answers.

Here are a few examples;

- What are you trying to achieve?
- Why is that important?
- What would be the perfect outcome?
- How are you going about it?
- Why do you do it that way?
- What could you do better?
- What obstacles are in the way?
- How could things be improved upon?
- How else have you considered doing it?
- What is the right thing to do?
- When does it need to be done by?
- What are the key milestones?
- Where is your chosen course of action likely to lead?
- What alternatives have you considered?
- Who is involved and why?
- Who else could be involved and why?
- What are the next steps?
- When will you start?
- How will you measure progress?
- How will you know that you have been successful?

Listen actively to the answers that you are given. Demonstrate your interest in the answers that you get by asking supplementary and relevant questions that challenge logic and reinforce understanding.

Have 'Me Days'

You will recall from Chapter 8 that one of the guidelines that I suggested would help you to survive in a corporate was to prioritise your activity. One of the first things that I started doing, once I had identified my boulders, was to put regular time aside in my diary, to concentrate on me.

I realised that it was going to take time for me to develop my brand as well as the associated behaviours that I needed to adopt and adapt to reinforce it. I committed to make appointments with myself in my schedule. I would treat these appointments with the same respect as those made with my customers or my bosses. In other words, I would only postpone or cancel them in exceptional circumstances.

I call these appointments 'Steve Days'. I am fortunate enough to do a job that enables me to spend full days on myself but in my earlier days I used to book one or two hour slots in my calendar. There are a couple of very important points to make about 'Me Days'. Firstly, if you don't make the appointment then you will never actually have the meeting. Secondly, you need to plan and prepare for how you will make best use of the appointment.

We all have a long mental list of things that we would like to do to improve ourselves. Hopefully, having completed the personal awareness analysis covered in Chapter 4 you may well feel that 'like to' should now read 'need to' and that your list is now tangible and written down in front of you rather than filed in the deep recesses of your subconscious. The problem is that we never actually get around to doing them because there always seems to be something more pressing which needs our attention. My provocation is that if we don't make the time that we will never make the improvements that we know we need to make. How mad is that? Talk about ever decreasing circles.

So, put some time aside in your diary and call it 'Me time'. Now look at what you need to do and plan and prepare for your first meeting accordingly. Ask yourself some questions.

What do I need to address and in what order? What will I address first? Why is it important? What information do I need to source in order to do it? Where, and or, from whom do I need to get it? Who can help me? What do I need to book in advance?

I have been having 'Steve Days' for over a decade now and I still have one at least once every month or so. I use them to read and research, to visit mentors, to attend training and development courses, to update my website. I use them to think.

Read more

I should read more books. Books are one of the greatest sources of knowledge. I placate myself with the notion that if I scan the odd business periodical and keep up with the news on television and in the newspapers that it will be ok. I've never been a great reader and often feel that only time that I have the opportunity to take on a 'whole book' is when I go on holiday. Then, as I kill the time between check-in and flight time, I scan the shelves of the bookshops in the airport desperately searching for something that looks interesting and merits accompanying me on my well earned down time.

The problem is that I often bail out and either pick up a trashy novel that holds me for about fifty pages, or buy nothing at all. So, I have adopted a new behaviour. I know that I will have time to read something on holiday so I buy a business book before I go and take it with me. I like business books because they are compartmentalised. You can select a chapter at random and then read and reflect. You don't have to take on the whole beast in one go and you can return to it whenever you wish.

I still read the newspapers of course. After all, they are a great source of immediate and up to date information. Crucial if you want to maintain and develop upon your commercial awareness. I used to read the newspaper backwards. I would start with the sport and then go to the headlines next. I would cover the rest if I had time. I have now adopted a new behaviour when it comes to reading the newspaper as well. I start with the business pages because I need to keep a handle on what is going on commercially. It is important to acquire a good grasp of what is currently happening in the City, in business generally and across the political landscape. Then I read the headlines and the sport if I have time.

Expand your vocabulary

Most people's vocabulary is remarkably limited. It is not only the range of vocabulary that some people are hampered by but also their ability to pronounce and articulate a wide range of words effectively. This may be driven by uncertainty as to the meaning of some words but I suggest that it is simply down to a lack of proactivity in seeking out new words and fully understanding their meaning.

In my view it is one of the easier ways that an individual can improve upon their personal impact. An improved vocabulary not only enables one to express oneself more effectively verbally but written work and emails become more concise, crisp and laconic.

I am fascinated by words and am in the habit of picking up a dictionary, almost on a daily basis and flicking through it. I stop randomly and pick a new word every day. I try to use it at least three times during the day in normal conversation in order to reinforce my learning and understanding of it. Even learning just one new word a day gives you another 365 ways of expressing yourself.

Confront your demons

As Eleanor Roosevelt once said, "You must do the thing you think you cannot do."

You may well have identified some of your potential areas of weaknesses when you completed the personal awareness analysis that we covered in Chapter 4. What is of vital importance is taking action to address those areas of personal development that are either affecting your performance or holding you back from further advancement. Ironically, most of us are well aware of the things that we need to address but singularly bad at doing anything about it.

Ninety per cent of the answer to effective personal development is recognising that something needs to be addressed. The remaining ten percent, doing something about it, however, is just as tough. It is amazing how often people will say that they will do something to address a weakness only to be saying the same thing months, or even years later.

We defer for any number of reasons. We may be afraid of failing, we may not have access to the tools, resources or people who can help or we procrastinate and put it off because we are too busy. Whatever the excuse, we know deep down inside that if we fail to take action then we will continue to be hampered by the fault. Put yourself in harm's way and take action by proactively addressing them one by one.

Create your own personal advert

What do you say when people ask how you are today? How would you mark your response out of 10? Do you say something like "Oh, mustn't grumble" or "Not too bad thanks"? What score would you give that out of 10 compared with; "Really good thanks" or, "I'm having a great day" or, "Bloody marvellous"? How you are actually feeling is not necessarily the point. It's the perception that you create with your answer that matters. Practice developing a personal suite of things that you always say and that you always do. You will become known for saying and doing them. Make them consistent with your beliefs, your values and your opinions.

You will be familiar with the old saying "Act in haste and repent at leisure." This is a behaviour that I have tried to stop.

Of course, most of the time our behaviours are entirely consistent with our brand. We usually have the time in which to consider how we will choose to react to an event. Every now and then however, we do not have that time and it is in these intense moments that the real us manifests itself. It is at these moments that my own Personal Brand Essence becomes so valuable to me. I simply remind myself of what it is before I choose my reaction.

Whatever you decide to do, do something. Take action now. It may take you some time to decide upon your full and final list of things to do and of course, it is an iterative process that will be ever evolving as a result, but the following provocation may help to start you on your way. It is based upon a model introduced to me by a good friend and former colleague of mine, Kieran Brady. He set himself the task of improving his work life balance and decided to take some proactive action to change some of his behaviours in order to redress what he thought was a balance tilted too much towards work.

Kieran contends that work life balance is a blend of four different elements: career, family, personal development and me.

Career is about our ambitions for career advancement, the company for whom we work, our role and the responsibilities and salary that come with it.

Family is about our home, where we live and socialise. It is about our friends and family and the things that we enjoy doing with them.

Personal development is about how we improve ourselves both in a work context through skills and experience development and in a personal context insofar as improving oneself as a person.

Me is all about having fun and staying healthy. It is very important to make time for ourselves, to remind ourselves of the things that we like doing and the importance of being fit and healthy enough to enjoy it.

There is factor that is common to all four components, that of our environment. Where we work geographically and the amount of travelling that we do, the company that we work for, its culture and the quality of its work space are all environmental factors that we need to take into account when deciding upon any changes in behaviour that we may make. Other environmental factors that we need to consider are where we live and the type of accommodation that we live in, whom we socialise with and where we socialise. We must get our environment right first in order to allow and enable us to focus on other factors. So, the question must be; What (if anything) do I need to do to improve my environment?

The following example highlights some of the promises that I made to myself to improve my own work life balance. Many of them became personal life goals for me and were incorporated into my own Personal Life Plan as a result.

135

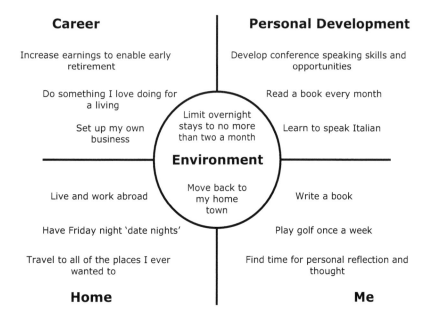

Career

Increase earnings to enable early retirement

Do something I love doing for a living

Set up my own business

Limit overnight stays to no more than two a month

Environment

Move back to my home town

Live and work abroad

Have Friday night 'date nights'

Travel to all of the places I ever wanted to

Home

Personal Development

Develop conference speaking skills and opportunities

Read a book every month

Learn to speak Italian

Write a book

Play golf once a week

Find time for personal reflection and thought

Me

Don't forget to set some timescales against each of your promises. This will help you to identify the steps that you need to take in order to realise them as well as help to prioritise and reality check the list.

So What?

- Brands live or die based upon how customers perceive the behaviours of the brand. The brand either reinforces the positive emotions that its customers have towards the brand or the customers walk away. The same applies to us as individuals. We must have a set of behaviours that are consistently representative of our own personal brand.

  - What do your behaviours say about you?
  - Are they consistent with creating the impression you desire?
  - What changes do you need to make?
  - What will you do differently to improve your environment?
  - How can you improve your work life balance?
  - What promises will you make to yourself?
  - What will be your new habits?
  - What will be your new behaviours?
  - When will you take the action that you need to take?
  - How will you measure the impact of those changes?

12

Brand through the line

"A rock pile ceases to be a rock pile the moment a single man contemplates it, bearing within him the image of a cathedral."
Antoine De Saint-Exupery

Shoes. I have a thing about shoes. I think that shoes say a lot about people and their personality. They are a detail that can often be overlooked. They are, in my view, highly symbolic of the care that an individual takes in their own personal appearance. My wife, Claire, thinks that I have an obsessive compulsive disorder when it comes to shoes. I am in the habit of cleaning them every time I remove them at the end of the day. I wrap them in the tissue paper that they were wrapped in when I first bought them and double them into the box in which they originally came. Every now and then I have a shoe cleaning fest and I take them all out of their boxes, unwrap them from the tissue paper, line them up and polish them all. Personally, I fail to see what her problem is. Every time I put on a pair of shoes they shine. Like new.

It wasn't always that way. Like most men I had three pairs of shoes. One black pair for work, one brown pair for the pub and a pair of sandals, as I chose to call them, for holidays. They were well worn-in and very comfortable. OK, they had a few scuffs on them and the heels were almost non-existent from the rigours of driving, but they did the job. My wardrobe fared similarly. It was packed with an eclectic mix of fashions from the preceding two decades. My suits were shinier than my shoes. My white shirts had turned a mysterious shade of grey. The collars curled slightly at the points and the cuffs were ragged. My ties looked great, well, for a Seventies fancy dress night at the local pub anyway. My belts were frayed and worn, due no doubt, to the over-straining that they were subjected to by my maturing waistline. I had a 34-inch waist when I was twenty and for some unfathomable reason was under the deluded misapprehension that I must therefore be about a 36-inch waist now that I had reached forty. I wasn't. The middle age spread had caught up with me and I was, in fact, a couple of sizes up from that. I became alarmed that my waist size was keeping pace with my age. Few of my clothes actually fitted me. Shirt collars set about trying to strangle me. Suit jackets gaped unattractively over my burgeoning chest and my ties clashed violently with my shirts.

There was a chasm between my business dress and the rest of my wardrobe. I used to go into cold sweats when invited to attend offsite work events where the required attire was described as 'smart casual'. The words would strike fear into my heart. My non-work wardrobe consisted of ill-fitting jeans and baggy, chunky tops. I didn't even own a tee-shirt, I was at least appreciative that these garments in particular did me no favours whatsoever. Polo shirts were to be worn when playing golf, Chino's were something to do with coffee and sports jackets were what my Grandad used to wear. Smart casual was usually a suit and a shirt with just the tie saved from another airing.

Then, one day, I saw myself in a conference video and the sight shocked me. I had worn my 'best stuff' because I knew that I was going to be on stage. I was over-weight and my clothes looked dreadful. I was running a business where I was constantly on show, whether that be selling to potential clients, delivering courses in front of groups of people or speaking at conferences with large audiences. I realised in that moment that the way that I looked was entirely inconsistent with the content of my messages, with the perceptions that I was trying to create and with my own Personal Brand Essence.

I decided to take some action. I lost some weight and just as importantly, I threw my wardrobe out, got over my vanity and bought some clothes that actually fitted me, realising that they were not only more comfortable to wear but that they made me feel good and essentially looked better as well. I didn't spend a fortune either. I choose to spend my money on travelling rather than the equivalent of a week in the sun on a pair of shoes, or a suit, or a pair of jeans. But then, each to their own. I bought new suits, new shirts and new ties, silk ties. I confronted the dreaded smart casual conundrum and gave my off-duty wardrobe a bit of a face-lift. Over time, I made sure that I had enough suits and smart casual outfits, all supported with their own pair of shoes, so that I could alternate them regularly. I adopted the habit of replacing my suits and shirts on a regular basis so that they always looked sharp and presentable and at least kept pace with fashion.

In the previous chapter we examined how your behaviours bring your brand essence to life but there is another vitally important aspect to creating the right impression. The way that you look has a fundamental effect on the opinions and perceptions that people first form of you. I know that we should never judge a book by its cover, but we do. We form perceptions of people the moment that we see them. The perception that we have formed is only enhanced or altered as we get to know them. It is human nature to do so. It is a basic animal instinct to draw conclusions from the way that others look. Peacocks would have a much easier time of it if that were not the case.

The way that you look is an essential part of your personal advert. It tells people, before you have even spoken, what you are all about. Marketers agonise about how their brand looks when they go above the line and into their customer's consciousness. They prevaricate over which adverts to run, through what media and which celebrities to use to endorse their products. Companies spend small fortunes on redefining themselves, renaming themselves and redesigning their logos and their colour schemes. All with good reason. It is the image that these things create that initially influences people's purchasing decisions.

Now, I am not about to give you a style lecture. I would be the first to admit that I am no fashionista, but what I do want to do is provoke you into thinking about how you look and the personal image that your look portrays.

We all have ensembles that we like to wear. I started to take note of what I had worn and when I had worn it. I engage with most of my clients on no more often than a monthly or quarterly basis as a rule. There is a distinct danger that I may end up wearing the same outfit each time I meet them unless I am aware of what I wore the last time that I saw them. Women are, in my experience, much better than men at recalling what they wore the last time they met somebody. Either way, it is important to think about what you wear and when you wear it, to mix and match as well as rotate your outfits in order to keep your appearance fresh and different.

Your clothes play an important part in the creation of your personal image, but they are not alone in creating the right impression. Your accessories play an equally important role. Your watch, your mobile phone, your diary, your pen, your handbag, your briefcase, your car and of course, your own personal hygiene and appearance, all add to the mix that people first notice when they meet you.

I remember pulling into a prospective client's car park in a courtesy car one morning. My company car was being serviced and as a result I wasn't driving the usual bells and whistles mobile. My client actually met me on the steps leading to the main entrance and saw me park the car. He commented on how pleased he was to see that the car I was driving wasn't a swanky, top of the line model that he would ultimately be paying for. It was another 'Aha' moment for me. It was the first time that I had really appreciated how people draw conclusions based on appearances – and the importance of first impressions. After our meeting he asked me for a lift to the station to save him from ordering a taxi. Once again I was left to reflect on what he would have thought if I had been in my own car which was invariably littered with clutter and saw a sponge and a duster once every couple of months.

That experience provoked me into considering many aspects of my own personal appearance and led to me asking myself a number of questions that, if I may, I will share with you to ponder upon as well.

- Do all of your clothes fit you?
- Are any of your belts showing the scars of another inch or two around the waist?
- Do you have any clothes hung up in your wardrobe that you haven't worn for over a year?
- Do you have any outfits that are more than three years old?
- Are your clothes appropriate for the work that you do?
- Are they of the right quality, cut, look and feel?
- Do you have sufficient suits to be distinct every day?
- Do you have a separate summer and winter wardrobe?
- Do your ties and scarves add colour and impact?
- Do all of your shoes look brand new?
- Do your handbags look brand new?
- Does your briefcase do you justice?
- What about your make-up and your hair?
- Is your perfume or aftershave suitable?
- What about your watch, your jewellery and your cuff-links?
- What about your pen and your day book?
- Is your personal organiser or diary looking a little battered?
- Is your mobile phone or personal computer a shade shabby?
- Is your ring tone compatible with your brand?
- Is your car clean, inside and out?

Take pride in your appearance and your personal image. It matters. Not only does it create a first impression that helps to form an initial perception, it creates an expectation.

So What?

- Having spent so much time identifying our Personal Brand Essence and the behaviours that you need to demonstrate in order to bring that brand to life, it would be a shame to spoil the ship for a ha'porth of tar.

- Businesses, quite rightly, spend vast amounts of money on ensuring that their products are promoted and packaged in the best possible way. As individuals we should also take the same time and care in paying attention to how we package and promote ourselves.

- Ask yourself these questions:
  1. What impression are you trying to create?
  2. What can you do to create greater impact through your personal appearance?
  3. What improvements can you make to your physical appearance?
  4. What improvements do you need to make to your wardrobe?
  5. What do your accessories say about you and your brand?

13

Building your commercial bandwidth

"The person who says it can't be done is generally interrupted by someone doing it."
Harry Emerson Fosdick

Picture a rainbow. We are all familiar with the spectrum of colours within a rainbow, a continuum from red through to violet. Each colour is distinct, miraculously differentiating from its neighbour. The array is phenomenal, the variety and assortment of colour, spectacular.

Compare a Cotswold stone wall, arching its way over the fields into the distance with a deep well boring into the earth on its search for water. One is a mile or more long but just a few feet in depth. The other is a mile or more deep but just a few feet across.

Commercial bandwidth is the spectrum of knowledge, awareness and understanding that an individual is able to call upon, benefit from and act upon in the course of conducting their business. Commercial bandwidth is business experience and know how that is a mile wide rather than a mile deep. Commercial bandwidth sets individuals aside from their peers and contemporaries. It enables them to act with more pace, more confidence and greater success because it draws upon that knowledge and experience.

Commercial bandwidth is business acumen. Commercial bandwidth is what people know and the experience to know what to do with that knowledge. It is experience that they have either had to learn through their own actions or knowledge that they have gleaned from the experiences of others. This is why personal networks are so important. They give us access to knowledge and experience, guidance and advice that we would otherwise not have.

I have talked a lot about commercial bandwidth through the course of this book. Rule 7 in Chapter 5 highlights the importance that mentoring plays in developing your commercial and personal bandwidth. You will recall from Chapter 7 that your Personal Development Plan should be designed to fill the gaps in your knowledge and personal skill set that enable you to legitimately reach for the next rung on the corporate ladder. In Chapter 8, I suggested that one of the ways in which you will survive and thrive in a business is to develop an understanding of the key business principles; another was to build a personal network. Many of the behaviours that I prompted you to consider adopting in Chapter 11 are designed to help build your commercial bandwidth. I want to share with you how I set about building my own commercial bandwidth in the hope that it will give you an insight into how you can grow yours.

Many of the people with whom I work on a one to one basis are already very successful. They have reached senior positions within their chosen companies. They are well established and well respected by their colleagues. They have achieved many of the things that they set out to do in their careers and many of them have a clear idea of what else they need to accomplish. Despite this, in some ways, they do not differ from a new starter in as much as they too come to a crossroads in their careers and are not certain of which direction to take next. They know that they have it within themselves, they just have a few blind spots as to how they will get there. Personal networks help to clear the mist and provide the clarity that people need in order to see which direction to take.

I wasn't certain where to begin. I already had a personal network of sorts. I had kept in touch with some of the people for whom and with whom I had worked during my career, though not in a

145

deliberate or structured way. Occasionally I would seek guidance and advice from them.

Then, one day I received a phone call. A new graduate had joined the business and he was flicking through our internal directory, looking for someone with sales and marketing experience. He was an IT specialist and had a degree in telecommunications. He also had the self-awareness to realise that he had little or no sales and marketing experience. He had the maturity to appreciate that one of the ways that he could fast track his knowledge of this was to sit down and spend time with someone who did. He asked if I could spare him an hour or so each month to help him. To be honest I was flattered that someone should have chosen me to help them in such a way. It never crossed my mind to say no. It was a small thing for me, but a huge thing for him.

I realised during the course of our conversation that I knew more about the subject than I had fully appreciated. The stories of successes and failures, the anecdotes and asides borne out of my own personal experiences were so much more powerful to him than the textbooks that he had read or the lectures that he had attended because they provided context, perspective and reality. I gained something equally as powerful. I began to appreciate that the most effective way to fill the gaps in my own Personal Development Plan was to seek out people who already had those skills and capabilities and to learn from them.

I revisited my Personal Development Plan and reminded myself of the gaps that I had between my current skills set and the capabilities that I needed to develop and be able to evidence in order to move onwards and upwards in the business. I began to list the people who I thought might be able to help. I looked within the business and outside of it as well. I looked for role models, recognised experts in their chosen fields, people that I had seen in action, who did the things that I needed to be able to do so much better than me.

I set about contacting them. Those that I knew and worked with I spoke with face to face. Those that I didn't, I called and wrote to. The message to all of them was the same. I had identified some personal weaknesses that I wanted to address. I needed to develop these capabilities because it would enable me to achieve what I wanted to do. I recognised that they had the skills that I needed to develop. I asked them if they would sit down with me for an hour or so a month and help me. Every single person I contacted agreed to do so. Thankfully, it is in our nature to want to help others. I guarantee that every single person you ask for help will agree to as well. You just need to ask them.

Creating a powerful personal network was the key for me. In creating my personal network I had also inadvertently created my own feedback circle. As time progressed and I began to appreciate the importance of others' assessment and evaluation of my performance. They all became, in one form or another, members of my 360 degree feedback circle. They encouraged me to find time for personal reflection and to be honest with myself in my assessment of how I was doing in brining my Personal Brand Essence to life. Because I had defined the actions that I would take and the behaviours that I would change and adopt I was able to measure my brand in action through their feedback on the changes that they had noticed.

My network needed to be a blend of people. I needed some people who could suggest alternative courses of action based upon their own experiences; I needed some people who were able to provoke me to think in a different way; I needed some people who would actively support me and put my ideas and suggestions forward on my behalf. My personal network needed to consist of coaches, mentors and sponsors.

It was important to me that I got a blend of objectivity as well as direct guidance. People from within the business were able to help me with specifics because they knew how the business worked, they understood the culture of the business and they knew the personalities involved. They were able to show and tell me what to do. They became my business coaches.

Others, often outside of the business, provided me with greater objectivity and impartiality simply because they didn't have a preconceived notion of the business. They were able to share their own experiences with me and ask more obvious questions of me. They were able to provoke me in a different way because they caused me to review even the fundamental ways that I addressed some of the day to day challenges that faced me. They became my personal mentors.

There were some whom I deliberately targeted because of who they were and where they sat in the business. They may have been in the position that I one day aspired to occupy. They may have been the boss of the person in that position. They were the key decision makers, the movers and shakers. I wanted to gain access to them not just to develop my own capabilities but to impress them with my ideas. I wanted their support and I wanted to harness that support to provide me with opportunity and open doors for me. It was still up to me to walk through the door and take advantage of those opportunities but it was these people who became my sponsors.

I needed to understand what it took to do the next job, so I spent time with people that currently did the role and asked them what it took to achieve the position and to do it well.

I needed to improve my presentation skills, create a better platform for my ideas and deliver them with greater impact, so I watched and learnt from those who did it well. I asked them how they prepared and came up with their ideas and managed their nerves.

I needed to increase my financial awareness and understand more fully the commercial levers that applied to my part of the business so I spent time with financial experts in the company and qualified accountants outside of it.

I needed to understand how others motivated their teams so I sought out the managers of teams that I could see were highly motivated. I asked them how they achieved it and what they suggested I could do to attain the same level of motivation within my team.

I needed to improve the content and structure of my website so I went to see the authors of those sites that I wanted to emulate.

I needed to learn how to make better use of the resources at my disposal, so I sought the knowledge and expertise of those who did more with less than I had at my disposal. I tried to understand and appreciate the different ways in which the same task can be approached.

I needed to improve sales performance by implementing a new sales process, so I gathered around me experts who had done it before and could show me the short cuts, what worked in theory and what actually worked in practise.

I wanted to set up my own business, so I spoke with people who had done so themselves in order to understand the pitfalls and risks involved in order that I could mitigate them as much as possible for myself.

And so the list continued and still does today. Your personal network has to evolve and change in line with your requirements. It has to be nurtured and protected. Ground rules around time, commitment and confidentiality need to be agreed. You must keep in touch with the people in your personal network, most especially when you have garnered what you wanted from them. Don' t forget the debt that you owe them. If you cannot pay them back directly, consider how you can make payment in kind by helping others that you can. Offer yourself as a coach, or a mentor, or a sponsor. As I have said before, you will gain even more from helping others.

Make time to discover. Make time to develop your commercial bandwidth. Make it one of your boulders, an integral part of your 'me days'. But also appreciate that it takes time. It is a process of osmosis. It happens over a long period of time and is something that is virtually impossible to measure on a day to day basis. It manifests itself more so on longer term reflection. When you compare what you know now and contrast it with what you knew a year or two ago.

So What?

- Commercial bandwidth is the spectrum of knowledge, awareness and understanding that an individual is able to call upon, benefit from and act upon in the course of conducting their business. Commercial bandwidth sets individuals aside from their peers and contemporaries. It enables them to act with more pace, confidence and success because it draws upon that knowledge and experience. It is experience that they have either had to learn through their own actions or knowledge that they have gleaned from the experiences of others.

- Commercial bandwidth is created though personal experience, research or from the knowledge and expertise of others. We do not have the time or opportunity to experience everything that we need to and this is why personal networks are so important. They give us access to knowledge and experience, guidance and advice that we would otherwise not have.

- Recognise the areas of knowledge and expertise that you would like to develop. Identify individuals who consistently demonstrate those skills and spend time with them.

14

Leadership through Personal Impact

"To every man there comes a time in his lifetime, that special moment when he is figuratively tapped on the shoulder and offered the chance to do a very special thing, unique to him and fitted to his talents. What a tragedy if that moment finds him unprepared or unqualified for the work that could be his finest hour."
Sir Winston Churchill

If there is one subject that has beguiled writers more than any other it is leadership. There is a pantheon of books on the subject written by management gurus, intellects as well as sporting and political celebrities. The definitions are boundless and the examples manifold. I have often mused as to whether our great leaders were born with the gift of great leadership skills or whether circumstance and fate forced them to hone and develop those skills.

I had determined that I would one day reach the position of General Manager within BT. I had worked my way up through the ranks and asked a former boss of mine, Simon Kelly, the man who introduced me to the concept of blue ocean strategy, for some advice as to how I could make the final leap required to secure the role. He gave me one of the best pieces of advice that I ever received. "Behave like one," he said. "Think like one and make decisions as though you were one." At the time I was less than convinced that this was going to be the enabler that I needed but what I found was that by implementing his advice people began to react to me and deal with me as though I was one. When I was officially appointed many people reacted in surprise, having assumed that I had been in the position for some time already.

Personally, I believe that great leaders are both born and made. I believe that everyone has the gift within them. What is required is either a conscious effort to bring the capabilities required to the fore or some set of circumstances that demand that someone assumes control. Either way the skills that are required can be learnt. Whether you, as an individual, have the desire to lead a team or the ambitions to manage a business is not the point. What is important is that you ensure that you create **personal impact** as an individual, that you make a difference and fulfil your full potential, be that at work or socially.

Leadership is a subject that has also fascinated me. I have read many books on the subject over the years. I have been fortunate enough to observe many fine leaders in action at first hand, both through business and sport. For me, leadership is a blend of defining and executing strategy.

Successful leaders inspire their followers by setting the vision and identifying the goals that need to be secured. They provide direction through the creation of a strategy and a plan to deliver those goals. They are skilled at communicating every element of the plan, using all of the communication channels at their disposal highly effectively. They ensure clarity and consistency by articulating the relevance and interdependency of the milestones of the plan. They drive execution by motivating their teams and the individuals within those teams through a clear understanding of what motivates them. They provide them with the reward and recognition required to incentivise them to achieve the goals stated in the strategy.

The literal definition of leadership, according to *The Oxford English Dictionary* is; Cause to go with one especially by guiding or showing the way or by going in front and taking a person's hand. My description of leadership does not only apply in the sense of leading a team. I contend that we are all leaders. We all guide or show the way through our actions and our behaviours. We all have it within us to 'go in front' or take the lead and set an example to others. I refer to it as leadership through Personal Impact.

All great leaders demonstrate the six key skills of leadership. Preparation, organisation, communication, motivation, inspiration and execution. These are also the key ingredients in creating Personal Impact. Personal Impact is created through the identification of one's own personal goals and the creation of a strategy, or plan, to ensure that those goals are achieved. Personal Impact is enhanced through the clear articulation of the individual's aims and aspirations as well as the ideas that enable them to be met. Personal Impact is reinforced by the motivation and inspiration of oneself and others. Personal Impact is evidenced through achievement. Nothing speaks more loudly than results.

Preparation

This is the first and the singularly most important element in achieving Personal Impact. I work with a man who sets his stall by the importance of good preparation. Stan Kaufman is the former Managing Director of Allders Department Stores and the Chairman of the *bssa* Oxford Summer School Committee. I have never met anyone who is more focused on the importance of preparation. For him it is the guiding principle behind any achievement. Its importance can never be underestimated. His attention to detail is quite mind boggling. His insistence upon contingency and scenario planning, legendary. But throughout his career it has got him results. Day after day, month after month and year after year. It gets him results.

There is a great quote, often attributed to Sir John Harvey-Jones but probably coined by John Preston, of Boston University that "the nicest thing about not planning is that failure comes as a complete surprise and is not preceded by a period of worrying and depression". Stan doesn't like surprises and neither should we, not when the strategy that we are constructing is the one for us. Defining our vision is the preparation that we must make and, at a personal level, our vision is defined by identifying the goals that we aim to achieve.

153

The good news is that you have already done this, well, if you identified your personal life goals in Chapter 6 that is.

Organisation

Creating the master plan comes next. Specifically, this means what are we going to do, how are we going to do it and when will we do it? This master plan becomes our strategy. It takes into account the resources that we have at hand and those that we need to acquire. It should be littered with milestones and measures to gauge our progress and reinforce our conviction that we are on the right track.

We all have the capacity for good organisation, whether that be planning a sales and marketing campaign at work or a day out with friends and family. After all, when was the last time that you jumped into the car without a clue as to how you would find your way to your destination? We plan all of the time, both consciously and subconsciously, from designing a new kitchen to hosting a dinner party, from managing our personal finances to booking our holidays. It is second nature to us. The same principles always hold true. What are we going to do? How are we going to do it? When will we do it? There is more good news. The Personal Life Plan that you have created and underpinned with your Personal Development Plan will form the foundation of your own master plan.

Communication

As I mentioned in Chapter 8, it is vitally important that we are able to communicate our ideas and opinions with clarity and impact. It is no coincidence that many of the world's great leaders are outstanding orators. They are able to impart their views with passion and in a way that moves people to take action. They have learned this art, through hours of coaching, practise and rehearsal. We can do the same. Many people struggle with how to structure and communicate their thoughts in a way that reinforces their Personal Brand Essence and maximises their impact.

Clarity of communication comes from being able to identify the single pure objective of the message. Ask yourself, what do you want your audience to know, or to do as a result of hearing your message? Do not be tempted to deviate from this basic principle. You must construct the content of your communication around one single point or else you run the risk of diluting your message or confusing your audience. In Chapter 15 I explain in more detail how I believe people can improve upon their communication skills when playing in the performance zone.

Motivation

You have probably always had a pretty good idea about what motivates you and the personal awareness analysis that you completed in Chapter 4 will hopefully have reinforced that. Like me, you may have found actually nailing down what your motivators are a little more difficult that you first thought however. This is because we have deliberately shifted it from our sub-consciousness into something that we can write down and clearly articulate. It isn't just about defining the things that motivate us; it is about determining how and why they motivate us. It is not easy but once we have our list it provides us with great clarity and purpose. We can decide to stop doing the things that demotivate us and take action to search out the opportunities to do the things that do.

People achieve things through other people. Ask yourself a question. Does your manager know what motivates you? If not, how can they possibly motivate you effectively? If you found it difficult to identify your own motivators what chance have they? If we take this further we can ask ourselves some more questions. Do you know what motivates the people that work for you? Do you know what motivates your friends? Do you know what motivates your loved ones? If you don't, how can you motivate and inspire them through your actions and behaviours? How can they help you achieve your goals?

Ask and tell. Make time to sit down with everyone who is important to you at work and at home to discuss your mutual motivations. If you understand what they want you can try to modify your behaviour to provide it. If they understand what you need they can attempt to do the same.

Inspiration

You are being watched. All of the time. Your managers monitor your performance. Your team seeks guidance from you. Your friends and acquaintances measure themselves against you. Your family looks up to you. You have to lead by example and try to be an inspiration to everyone all of the time in both thought and indeed. It isn't easy and it certainly isn't something that I would suggest should be in your consciousness all of the time, but it is important that we are more self-aware. It is what I mean by living your brand. Over time, the new habits and behaviours that you form will become second nature to you.

Involve people in your thought processes and your decisions both socially and professionally. People will be more proactively involved if they feel that they have been consulted and that their views and opinions have at least been taken into consideration, even if you decide not to act upon all of them. Demonstrate your trust for others by delegating ownership and allowing their ideas and suggestions to come to the fore, to build upon your own.

Execution

Ultimately it is the outcome against which we are measured. Once we have decided to do something we must see it through to completion. That does not mean that we do not take stock as we implement our plans. It is a sign of maturity that we are prepared to admit that we have got something wrong or are prepared to alter course. What is important is that this does not happen too frequently.

Thorough research and preparation will minimise the times that this happens. Through research and preparation we form an understanding of the scope of task at hand. We can then explore alternative courses of action and make an informed decision about which option to take. Before we take action we need to ensure that we have identified the key performance indicators that will demonstrate that it is being implemented successfully and having the desired effect. We can measure progress and collect evidence as we proceed as well as refine or even change the plan if we need to.

You know what your vision for your future is. You have identified your own personal life goals and created a Personal Life Plan and a Personal Development Plan. You know how to communicate your opinions and your ideas. You are clear as to your own motivation and have a greater appreciation of how to motivate and inspire others around you. You know what has to be done. Now all you need to do is follow your bliss. Go and do what you need to do.

So What?

- There are six key elements to leadership.

  1. Preparation
  2. Organisation
  3. Communication
  4. Motivation
  5. Inspiration
  6. Execution

- Leadership is a blend of defining and executing strategy. Successful leaders inspire their followers by providing direction and creating the goals that need to be secured in order to deliver the big idea, the objectives of the business.

- They are skilled at communicating every element of the plan, using all of the communication channels at their disposal highly effectively. They ensure clarity and consistency by articulating the relevance and interdependency of the milestones of the plan.

- They drive execution by motivating their teams and the individuals within those teams through a clear understanding of what motivates them. They provide them with the reward and recognition required to incentivise them to achieve the goals stated in the strategy.

15

Playing in the Performance Zone

"The harder I practice, the luckier I get."
Gary Player

There is a place, on a stage, that I call the performance zone. The performance zone is the place where your entire energy is concentrated on the interaction with the audience. Where the skills being exercised have been shifted to the subconscious. Where the experience is created.

In the context of delivering a speech or a lecture the performance zone differs significantly from the presentation zone. Most people, when delivering a presentation are focused on the presentation itself, trying to manage their nerves, worrying about the technology and trying not to fluff their lines. They are not performing, they are presenting. Their focus is on finishing not relishing the moment.

It is worth pointing out that many people don't ever reach the presentation zone. In a recent survey of undergraduates respondents were asked what they were most frightened of. Presenting in public to their peers came second. Dying came third. Evidently, people would rather die than present in public!

The question is, of course, what are they frightened of? After all, we were all born with just two innate fears, the fear of falling and the fear of noise. These fears are understandable as they signify danger and trigger our natural survival instincts. Why then are we afraid of the dark? Why are we afraid of change? Why are we afraid of

159

competition? Is it fear of the unknown, or fear of failure or embarrassment?

We have become conditioned, often by seeing others 'fail', to avoid the situations that give rise to these anxieties. The problem is, that unless we confront these fears and overcome them we will not be able to practice our skills and create the experiences that become our personal anchors. These build the courage that we need in order to be brave enough to do what we know needs to be done.

Performance creates confidence. Throughout this book, I hope to have provoked you to consider what you need to do in order to improve yourself. By now you will have a long list of things to do. Personal goals to achieve, strengths to build upon, weaknesses to address, new skills to develop, new behaviours to adopt and new people to contact.

My point is, that if we fail to address these things because we are afraid of failing then we will achieve nothing. My own experiences teach me that most of them are actually surprisingly easy to achieve. Each success builds confidence. Each attempt builds experience. Each incidence creates a personal anchor that reinforces self-belief. Practice makes perfect and the more we can practice the new skills that we are trying to develop, the more effective those skills will be, especially when the time comes for us to use them in anger. Put yourself in harm's way and learn from your mistakes as well as your successes. If we don't try how will we know?

Much of this book addresses the importance of managing one's own attitude and I make no apology for that. I passionately believe that if people demonstrate the right attitude then everything else will follow. That said, it is critical that people also develop the skills needed in order to succeed. Attitude plus skills enables performance. By definition skills can be taught and learnt and it is of paramount importance that we practice and perform these skills as often as we can in order to develop and progress, both personally and professionally.

Most people benefit from a similar education. Most people share the same qualifications, business knowledge and life experiences as their contemporaries at work. I believe that one of the few ways that people can actually differentiate themselves from their competitors is by being able to articulate their thoughts in a well structured and impactful way. As I mentioned earlier, most people would rather die than present in public. By the way, just in case you were wondering, the number one fear of the undergraduates surveyed was the death of a loved one. I believe that if we are able to develop, enhance and improve upon our presentation skills it gives us a distinct advantage.

I used to hide when the opportunity to deliver a presentation arose. I would often be involved in strategic planning days and disappear, off-site, with other members of the management team for a day or so. These events usually entailed a number of small breakout groups working through a problem or business issue. I was always actively involved in the breakout session but when the time came to present back the group's findings to the wider audience my eyes would search for the floor and my hands stay firmly down. I was afraid of making a fool of myself in front of my colleagues and my bosses. I was afraid of damaging my brand. The irony was, of course, that by not putting myself in harm's way I was causing more damage to my brand and my reputation. The same few people used to stand up and present the findings of their breakout group. They became personally associated with ideas that the group as a whole had come up with. Their opinions were sought on the subject by my bosses. They were usually asked to implement the ideas, often with a promotion and pay rise to boot.

I realised that if I was going to progress, both personally and professionally, I needed to confront this demon. I needed to put myself in harm's way and learn how to present effectively. Over the years, despite my anxieties and nerves, I have continually practised this skill, often when I didn't have to. I wanted to hone my skills to the point that when the time came that I had to deliver an outstanding presentation I had the confidence, through the experiences I had gained and the personal anchors that I had created, to do so.

Perhaps surprisingly, there are very few secrets to successful public speaking. For me, there are just three, preparation, structure and rehearsal.

You will recall from the previous chapter that when you are planning and preparing a presentation you need to be focus on the needs of your audience and be very clear about the single pure objective of your presentation. Once that is established you can set about structuring your message.

You will know that all forms of communication should have a beginning, middle and end. The challenge that I believe many people face is deciding what to put in each of these parts. I have used a simple model to structure all of my messages for many years now, whether they are written or verbal. The same principles apply for a sales call, an article on a website, an invitation to a party, a phone call, a management briefing or a presentation.

Your opening should include a synopsis and an opportunity statement. It is critical that you open your message with impact and that you grab your audience's attention right at the start. Consider using something like a shocking newspaper headline, or an amazing fact or a thought provoking quotation. The synopsis is designed to bring your audience up to speed. It should account for around 10% of the total time or length of the overall message. It is here that you ensure that everyone gains a common understanding of what you are going to talk about and that they all have a basic appreciation of your subject matter. It is where you remind them of the 'As Is' situation, the way that things currently are.

The opportunity statement comes next and accounts for around 15% of the overall message. Here you paint a picture of the future, the 'To Be'. You encourage your audience to imagine what a different future could look like by painting pictures for them and proffering alternative scenarios.

Your bridge to the main body of your presentation, the middle, is where you state the single pure objective of your message.

It is in the middle of your presentation that you explain the detail behind the opportunities that you have just outlined. You describe how your vision of the future will be implemented and detail the action that is required. It should account for around 70% of the total content as it explains the how and the when of your message. It is where you bring the opportunity to life.

The close of your presentation accounts for just 5% of the overall content. Nonetheless, it is just as vital as the rest. It is your sign-off, a reinforcement of everything that you have already said. It is the final peal of the bell that you want ringing in your audience's ear. Here you describe to them the benefits that they will enjoy as a result of implementing your vision of the future. Of what they will get when we arrive at the destination that you have illustrated. It is where you provide options and suggest alternative courses of action. It is where you seek endorsement for your idea and their commitment to implementing your recommendations.

A suggested model to use when structuring a presentation or planning any form of communication.

The Synopsis

- Around 10% of the overall presentation
- Give background to bring people up to speed
- Provide context and relevance
- Describe the 'As Is' situation
- Ensure a common understanding

The Opportunity

- Around 15% of the overall presentation
- Excite your audience with a view of the future
- Use metaphors to create a theme and thread
- Describe the 'To Be' situation
- Use words like 'picture' and 'imagine'

The Bridge

- The single pure objective of your message

The Method

- Around 70% of the overall presentation
- Describe how we will get there
- Detail the action that will need to be taken
- Identify timescales and key milestones
- Bring the opportunity to life

The Benefits

- Around 5% of the overall presentation
- Describe what we will get when we arrive
- Reinforce the benefits outlined in the opportunity
- Explain what is in it for them
- Give options and seek commitment

Example 1. Structuring a business update

Note: Who are your audience and what do they need/want to hear?

The Synopsis

- Current performance highlights and lowlights
- Current business issues and their impact on performance
- Top three challenges currently faced

The Opportunity

- Current key focus areas to improve performance of the team and individuals
- The benefits that the desired outcome will bring to the business

The Bridge

- The specific activity planned to deliver the desired outcome

The Method

- Detail the specific actions planned in order of priority
- Highlight the key milestones, dependencies and interdependencies
- Identify the resources required

The Benefits

- Make a commitment to deliver
- Request support or resources if required
- Give options and seek commitment

Example 2. Structuring a personal advert for an interview

Note: Who are your audience and what do they need/want to hear?

The Synopsis

- Who are you? Supported with three fascinating facts
- What motivates you?
- What are you looking for in the new opportunity?

The Opportunity

- Outline the capabilities that you would bring to the job
- Give your career highlights
- Describe the experiences and successes of your previous roles

The Bridge

- The difference that makes you the difference – your brand promise

The Method

- Detail your CV in reverse chronological order
- Highlight key areas of responsibility, targets and people
- Talk about your personal and social interests

The Benefits

- What are the 3 things that you will bring to their business or the new role?
- Why should they choose you ahead of the other candidates?
- Seek commitment to you

Example 3. Structuring an after dinner speech

Note: Who are your audience and what do they need/want to hear?

The Synopsis

- Open with a relevant story, anecdote or quotation
- Introduce yourself
- Tell your audience what you are going to talk about

The Opportunity

- Intrigue your audience
- Give your point of view
- Explain why people should listen to you
- Describe what they will get from listening to you

The Bridge

- The single pure objective of your speech

The Method

- Detail what needs to happen
- Explain why it needs to happen
- Indicate when it needs to happen

The Benefits

- Describe how people will feel, physically and emotionally by doing it
- Explain the benefits that they will get from doing it

166

We all know a good joke, right? One that we keep up our sleeves for those nights out with friends. You will recall, no doubt, the first time that you heard the joke that you now call yours. Remember the first time that you told it? How did it go? It probably wasn't seamless. You may have forgotten a couple of details, or worse still, missed something crucial out. The next time you told the joke it probably went a little better. Over time you start adding little asides and pauses for effect. You now mimic the characters and even adopt their accents. You have learnt the joke. You don't walk around with the joke written down on a piece of paper that you produce at the opportune moment. You have taught your brain the joke. When you next tell it your brain will deliver it to you all neatly packaged up, because it knows what you are going to say. You deliver the joke in the performance zone, not the presentation zone.

It amazes me how many people attempt to deliver a speech or a lecture or a presentation without having first rehearsed it. They have prepared thoroughly, kept their audience in mind when selecting the theme and thread, and selected the words that they know will resonate with them. They have structured the presentation around a single pure objective. They have an opening that grabs the audience's attention and a close that moves them to action. Then they stand up and expect to deliver it with impact. Learn the joke. Rehearse over and over again. It is only when you are confident of being able to stand up and deliver the presentation without your notes that you can play in the performance zone. That is not to say that you shouldn't use your notes, of course you can. It is to say that you should be able to deliver it without them if you had to.

I present now, almost every day. I still have a lot to learn but every time I do present I increase my experience and create personal anchors for myself. I still get nervous before big stage shows but I know that I can do it, because I have done it before. I pull on my personal anchors.

The stage is my performance zone, but then so is the boardroom when I am pitching to a client, or the classroom when I am working with a group. I try out new things. I put myself in harm's way. I sense the effects and try to improve upon them. It is how we all build experience and skill. It is how we all get results. It is how we improve and develop ourselves.

So What?

- The performance zone is where experience is created. It is vital in our journey of personal development that we develop and practice the skills that will enable us to succeed. Performance creates confidence. Our challenge is to overcome the fear of failing in order to realise our ambitions.

- Some points for you to ponder:
  1. Confront your fears
  2. Attitude plus skills enable performance
  3. Practice makes perfect
  4. Create experiences that become personal anchors
  5. Be brave and put yourself in harm's way
  6. If we don't try how will we know?

Conclusion

"There is no obstacle you cannot surmount, no challenge you cannot meet, no fear you cannot conquer, no matter how impossible it may sometimes seem."
Erin Brockovich

As I have written this book, words have begun to hold an even greater fascination to me. I once read somewhere that there are over 600,000 words in the English language, almost twice as many more words than in any other language in the world. If this fact isn't staggering enough what amazed me is that the average person has a vocabulary range of about 40,000 words, less than ten percent of the words available to them. I'd like to think that my vocabulary range has improved a little as a result of writing this book and I thank goodness for the *Oxford English Dictionary and Thesaurus* for helping me to achieve that. But I want to leave you with one final thought. A thought that is made up of just ten words, each of which consists of only two letters.

If it is to be it is up to me.

This phrase is reputed to have been coined by Bob Torrance, a much revered mentor and coach in that most frustrating of games and father of the great Ryder Cup golfer Sam Torrance. When I first heard the phrase it rang through my head like the peal of a great bell. It summed up everything to me. How many people do we know who sit and wait for things to happen for them? How many people do we know who seem to complain about everything because of 'the way they are placed'? How many people do we know who simply do not take responsibility for themselves, their actions or their lives?

If it is to be it is up to me.

What a mantra! Hopefully, nobody forced you at gunpoint to read this book and if you have read this far then I am sure that I am talking to a convert, but what you do as a result of reading this book is ultimately your responsibility.

You have the opportunity to understand yourself more fully.

You have an opportunity to take action to improve yourself.

You have the opportunity to identify the personal goals that you most want to achieve.

You have the opportunity to create a Personal Life Plan to enable you to realise those dreams and aspirations.

You have the opportunity to construct a relevant and focused Personal Development Plan.

You have the opportunity to decide upon what you will do to make a difference.

You have the opportunity to define your own Personal Brand Essence.

You have the opportunity to adopt the behaviours that reinforce and best represent your brand.

You have the opportunity to build a personal network designed to broaden your commercial bandwidth and your personal credibility.

You have the opportunity to demonstrate leadership by creating a platform for your ideas and delivering them with personal impact.

You have the opportunity to create your plan, to make a promise to yourself and to deliver upon it.

Whether you do any or all of them is, of course, entirely your decision. All I can do is hope that I have provoked you to take some action based upon what it did for me.

If it is to be it is up to me.

Further information

Created in 2004 by Steve Connell, *inspire* is a management development consultancy that focuses on the delivery of development programmes to talent pools identified by clients, one to one coaching and conference speaking. Steve specialises in the subjects of Personal Brand Essence and Business to Business account management. He also runs workshops that are open to all, on Presentation Skills and Selling Skills.

The *inspire* client list is extensive and we enjoy good relationships with organisations from many market verticals.

inspire delivers courses on:

- Personal Brand Essence
- Professional Presentation Skills
- Sales Account Management
- Leadership
- Effective Management
- Commercial Awareness
- The Principles of Selling
- The Principles of Marketing

For further information on inspire please visit: *www.inspiretalent.co.uk*

To join the Personal Brand Essence community of interest network please visit *www.personalbrandessence.com*

To order further copies of this book please visit *www.personalbrandessence.com*

To find out more about the *bssa* Oxford Summer School please visit *www.bssa.co.uk*

Recommended further reading:

Go for it! – Helen Exley

Breakthrough to Peak Performance – Jim Steele, Colin Hiles and Martin Coburn

People don't buy what you sell; they buy what you stand for – Martin Butler with Simon Gravatt

The Oxford Dictionary of Quotations – Oxford University Press

Marketing Management – Philip Kotler

The 7 Habits of Highly Effective People – Stephen R. Covey

Blue Ocean Strategy – W. Chan Kim and Reneé Mauborgne

Acknowledgements

There is a danger that this part of the book could end up as an entire chapter in itself. I have been influenced by so many people throughout my career and my personal life that I am hesitant to even start trying to list those who have played a part in provoking the thoughts which I have attempted to gather together in this book, for fear of forgetting to mention somebody. So I will limit my name checks to those whom I have referenced in the book, those whose provocations were running through my mind as I wrote the book and those who helped me to get the book from an entry in my own Personal Life Plan into the form that you now see it. I owe a huge debt of thanks to many other people, including my friends, my family, my clients and many former colleagues.

I must begin by mentioning Martin Butler and Neil Kennedy, two relentless supporters of the Oxford Summer School. It was from them that I first heard the term 'Brand Essence' and it was their outstanding articulation of what that meant in the context of business brands that initially set my train of thought on its way.

My mentors: Steve Clarke, Carolyn Elson, Stan Kaufman, Jim Lawless, Greg Philips.

Writers and coaches who have influenced me: Martin Butler, Stephen Covey, Helen Exley, Philip Kotler, Jim Lawless, Andrew Lothain, Dave Meckin, Jim Steele, Richard Ward.

The three most outstanding managers for whom I have worked: Graham Hibbard, Simon Kelly, Colin Mattey.

Nick Dale-Harris and the team at Management Books 2000 Ltd.

Lindsey Braune – Final draft proofing.

Stan Kaufman – Editorial comment and Preface.

Cheryl Owen – Publishing guidance.

My band of 'proofers' who spotted my glaring typo's and corrected my amazing propensity to misspell even the shortest of words; Helen Badlam, Bridget Berrecloth, Louise Cooper and Carolyn Folley.

To everyone who took the time to read the final draft of the book and provide feedback, comment and invaluable advice. In particular, Kieran Brady, Steve Clarke, Mark Higgins, Joanne Hopwood and Simon Kelly.

The Concise Oxford Dictionary for its definitions and help with spelling. Wikipedia, the superb online Encyclopaedia. Microsoft Word and its marvellous Thesaurus.

I must conclude with Claire, my wife and my inspiration, for her unwavering support and her total belief in me, without whom I would never have had the courage to begin.

Index

Last word

"We will not know unless we begin", said the eminent American Historian and Political Scientist, Howard Zinn. So here, in a page, is a summary of this book. Have fun and good luck!

Be very, very clear about what you want to stand for.
Be very, very clear as to why that it is important to you.
Be very, very clear about what that will enable you to do.
Get your attitude right.
Define your personal goals.
Create a plan that enables you to achieve them.
Make promises to yourself and keep them.
Develop the skills that you need.
Build confidence in yourself.
Put yourself in harm's way and play in the Performance Zone.
Grow your self-belief.
Create personal anchors for yourself.
Be brave and have the courage of your convictions.
It is time to begin...